Art & Theory of
SELF-DEFENSE

ABRIDGED

Hidehiko (Hidy) Ochiai

SELF-DEFENSE CURRICULUM

Third Edition

Ochiai, LLC
Lansdowne

Copyright © 2022, 2019, 2018 by Ochiai, LLC

Art & Theory of Self-Defense – Third Edition

All rights reserved. Printed in the United States of America.

NO PART OF THIS PUBLICATION may be:

reproduced or transmitted in any form or by any means, electronic or mechanical,
including photocopy, recording, or any information storage
or retrieval system now known or to be invented,
without permission in writing from the publisher.

ISBN: 978-0-9993979-6-1

HIDY OCHIAI

*"My true role is that of a 'teacher.'
My subject is human development, as it allows
people to live together harmoniously."*

~Hidy Ochiai

Hidy Ochiai, a native of Japan and an U.S. citizen, came to the United States in 1962 with the mission of teaching the martial arts. In 1966, after receiving his B.A. from Albright College, Master Ochiai moved to Binghamton, NY and established Wa-Shin Ryu (*wa*–harmony, *shin*–truth) Karate-do in the United States. Wa-shin Ryu now includes many branch schools across the United States.

From 1967-1980, Master Ochiai established himself as one of the world's premier martial artists. He was rated the number one kata (form) competitor by the PKA (Professional Karate Association), having won the United States Grand National Karate Championship for five consecutive years, an unduplicated record. He has been inducted twice to the Black Belt Magazine's Hall of Fame in 1979 as "Instructor of the Year" and in 1980 as "Man of the Year." In 2004, Hidy Ochiai was inducted to the Martial Arts History Museum's Hall of Fame in Los Angeles. His accomplishments have been praised by the media nationally and internationally including Black Belt Magazine, and ABC's Wide World of Sports, and ESPN.

As a pioneer in the field of character education, in 1994 Hidy Ochiai founded the non-profit organization called the Educational Karate Program (EKP), which was validated by the NYS Education Department as a program suitable for all public schools in New York State. EKP, which is now known as Educational Self-defense (ESD), teaches students of all ages an attitude of respect, confidence, anti-drugs and anti-violence. ESD has certified more than 1700 teachers in the public schools.

Hidy Ochiai is the author of five books, including several comprehensive texts on self-defense, the most recent of which is *Art and Theory of Self-Defense* (2017, 2019, 2022). His acclaimed book, *A Way to Victory: Miyamoto Musashi's Book of Five Rings* is an English translation and commentary of Musashi's ancient text and represents a seven-year effort to render the wisdom and spirit of Musashi's timeless teachings. First released in Japan, *A Way to Victory* was republished in the U.S by Overlook Press.

Hidy Ochiai's humanitarian efforts have been recognized worldwide. On November 1, 2002, the Japanese Government honored Master Ochiai as "an ambassador" of traditional Japanese culture and art. His Excellency, Ryozo Kato, the Ambassador of Japan, recognized Hidy Ochiai during the Embassy's celebration of Japan's Culture Day, which was held at the Ambassador's residence in Washington, D.C. Master Ochiai was one of twelve traditional martial arts masters chosen by the Japanese government to receive this honor and recognition. In 2005, Master Ochiai was elected chairman of the Japanese Masters Association of North America. As chairman, he produced a historic world premiere performance by the Japanese Masters Association's founding members at the Performing Arts Center Purchase College—State University of New York in October 2007.

In 2001, Hidy Ochiai founded the Hidy Ochiai Foundation, which encompasses the philosophy of his lifelong teachings, the basis of which is expressed in the dynamic relationship between the mind and the body. With training, the mind and the body become unified in such a way that the individual becomes the true master of the self. Dedicated to promoting the principles of non-violence, the Hidy Ochiai Foundation focuses on helping children and young adults learn to practice a positive and peaceful way of life, based on respect, self-discipline, self-confidence and mental and physical health. It is the Hidy Ochiai Foundation's mission to help people become constructive citizens, living in harmony with others.

In the pursuit and expression of his art, Hidy Ochiai's fundamental aim has been to help individuals walk the path of self-development with dignity.

Introduction

It is the nature of a human being to grow. To thwart the natural process of growth is to cloud the spirit and to endanger one's life. Recently, a 10-year-old child asked me, "Why do we need to practice self-defense?" I answered, "Because you are important, because your life is valuable." Training in self- defense offers a path of continuous development, which engages the total self – body, mind and spirit. As a person grows, he or she can apply this increasingly evolved self to contribute to society, while defining one's place in the world.

In this book, *Art and Theory of Self-defense*, essential training methods are presented to guide individuals toward proficiency in self-defense, as well as to a path of inner development. The highest form of self-defense lies in how we handle every day, moment-to-moment decisions. Our primary task is to live each moment well and in the best way that we possibly can. True mastery of this art lies in the countless moments before the execution of a physical, life-saving technique.

As a teacher, my obligation is to offer correct tools for growth and training in self-defense. Many of these tools are interwoven and interdependent. Such as, *kaizen* (constant improvement) – a word that historically has only applied to industry in Japan – can be applied effectively as an important tool in self-defense training. Central to the practice of *kaizen* is the word "constant." To constantly improve, one must develop awareness through *sho-shin* (beginner's mind) and strengthen willpower through *nin-tai* (patience and perseverance).

If one is committed to right practice in self-development, inevitably it will guide one to the right path with others. Certain principles promote harmony with the world, such as respect, non-violence, compassion, integrity and sincere stewardship of one's life—this is known as The Way.

 It is my earnest hope that this book will contribute to each person developing his or her true potential. The path of growth, ultimately, is the path of peace.

Contents

1	**Self-defense in Context**	P. 1

Historical Perspective of Non-violence and Self-defense
    STORY INSERT #1: *The Tale of Bokuden*

2	**Fighting Arts and Self-defense in Ancient History**	P. 5
3	***Ji-ei Jitsu*** **(Self-defense) ~ *To-Te* (Chinese Hand) ~ *Do* (Way)**	P. 11

Section 1 – The Ryukyu Kingdom: Self-defense and Non-violence
Section 2 – Definition of Non-violence and the Choice of Peace for the Individual
Section 3 – Distinction between Self-defense and Martial Arts

4	**The Study of Self-defense and Individual Development**	P. 17

Section 1 – The Mind-Body Connection Theory: The Heart of Self-defense Training
    STORY INSERT #2: *Belief and Confidence: A Musashi Anecdote*
Section 2 – Upward Spiral: Development of Positive Character Traits through Self-defense Training
Section 3 – Definition of a "Strong Person" and STORY INSERT #3: *The Tale of The Tea Master*

5	**Perception or "Seeing" in Self-Defense: *Ken* and *Kan* (Levels of Self-defense)**	P. 29

STORY INSERT #4: *A Kind Word Turneth Away Wrath*
Section 1 – Level One: Mental Self-defense (The Advanced Guard)
Section 2 – Level Two: Establishing Distance from Perceived Danger
Section 3 – Level Three: Surviving Physical Assault

6	**Attitude in Training**	P. 37

Section 1 – Culture and Regimen of the Training Hall and *Self-defense Creed*
Section 2 – *Sho-shin*
Section 3 – *Nin-tai*: Determination to Practice with Patience and Perseverance
Section 4 – *Kaizen*: Importance of Constant Improvement and Self-Competition
Section 5 – Intention: "Practice as if it's real."
Section 6 – Safety

7	**The Breath, Energy and *Ki-ai***	P. 43

Section 1 – Importance of Breath
Section 2 – Practice of *Mokuso* (Quiet Body, Quiet Mind): Preparing the Mind for Training
Section 3 – Standing Breathing Technique (Preparation and Practice)
Section 4 – *Tanden*
Section 5 – *Ki-ai*: Definition, Practice and Use

8	**Basic Format for Self-defense Training Sessions**	P. 49

Section 1 – Class Format for Teaching Self-defense to Children in a School Setting
Section 2 – Class Format for Teaching Self-defense to Adults

9	**Stances (*Tachikata*)**	P. 53

Section 1 – Elements of a Strong and Proper Stance
Section 2 – Attention Stance (*Musubi-dachi* and *Heisoku-dachi*)
Section 3 – Attention Stance and Bow (*Rei*)
Section 4 – Natural Stance (*Shizen-tai* or *Hachiji-dachi*)
Section 5 – Parallel Stance (*Heiko-dachi*)
Section 6 – Front Stance (*Zenkutsu-dachi*)
Section 7 – Straddle Stance or Horse Stance (*Kiba-dachi*)
Section 8 – Sumo Stance or Stamping Stance (*Shiko-dachi*)
Section 9 – Back Stance (*Kōkutsu-dachi*): Variations 1-2
Section 10 – Half-and-Half Stance (Modified *Fudo-dachi*)
Section 11 – One-Step-Forward Stance (*Moto-dachi*) and Practice of *Zan-shin*

10 Strengthening the Mind-Body Connection — P. 67

Section 1 – The Mind-Body Connection Exercise
Section 2 – Simple Walking Exercise Joined with Breathing (*Doh-zen*)
Section 3 – *Jufu Kihon*
Section 4 – *Jufu no Kata Godan (Ichi)*

11 The Fist — P. 81

Section 1 – Self-Power (*Ji-riki*): The Significance of the Fist in the Mind-Body Connection
Section 2 – Making the Traditional Fist or Fore-fist: Two Methods

12 Striking Surfaces and Striking Targets — P. 85

Section 1 – The Hands
Section 2 – The Feet
Section 3 – Striking Targets: Front of the Human Body
Section 4 – Striking Targets: Back of the Human Body

13 Blocking — P. 93

Section 1 – Upper Block (*Age-uke*)
Section 2 – Middle Striking Block (*Uchi-uke*)
Section 3 – Middle Inside/Outside Block (*Soto-uke*)
Section 4 – Down or Downward Block (*Gedan-barai*)
Section 5 – Wedge Block (*Kakiwake-uke*)
Section 6 – Cross Block or X-Block: Upward and Downward (*Juji-uke*)
Section 7 – Scooping Block (*Sukui-uke*)
Section 8 – Open Hand Half-Circle Block (*Kaisho Han-en uke*)
Section 9 – Knee Block (*Hiza-uke*)

14 Punching and Striking: The Use of Hands and Arms in Self-defense — P. 105

Section 1 – Practice of Punching and Important Elements of a Correct Punch
Section 2 – Traditional Punch: Fore-fist Straight Punch (*Seiken-choku-zuki*)
Section 3 – Traditional Punch in Front Stance: Lunge Punch (*Oi-zuki*) /Reverse Punch (*Gyaku-zuki*)
Section 4 – Practice of Striking
Section 5 – Back-Fist Strike (*Ura-Ken Uchi*)
Section 6 – Elbow Strikes (*Empi-uchi*)
Section 7 – Application of Elbow Strikes
Section 8 – Spear Hand Strike (*Nukite*)
Section 9 – Palm Heel Strike (*Teisho-uchi*)

15 Kicking and Striking: The Use of Feet and Legs in Self-defense — P. 125

Section 1 – Benefits and Mechanics of Kicking and Striking with Feet and Legs
Section 2 – Front Kick (*Mae-geri*)
Section 3 – Front Kick (*Mae-geri*): Stepping to Front Kick Practice
Section 4 – Side Kick (*Yoko-geri*)
Section 5 – Roundhouse Kick (*Mawashi-geri*)
Section 6 – Back Kick (*Ushiro-geri*)
Section 7 – Stamping Kick (*Fumikomi-geri*)
Section 8 – Front Knee Kick (*Mae-hiza-geri*)
Section 9 – Roundhouse Knee Kick (*Mawashi-hiza-geri*)

16 Kata (Form) — P. 139

Section 1 – Introduction to Kata
Section 2 – *Kihon Kata Sho-dan* (Basic Kata #1): Right and Left (*Migi* and *Hidari*)
Section 3 – *Kihon Kata Ni-dan*
Section 4 – *Kihon Kata San-dan* and *Yon-dan*: Line of Performance ("*Enbusen*")
Section 5 – *Kihon Kata San-dan*
Section 6 – *Kihon Kata Yon-dan*

17 Blocker Training Methods   P. 157

Section 1 – Blocker Technique 1: Wall of Confidence
Section 2 – Blocker Technique 2: Upper Block and Front Kick
Section 3 – Blocker Technique 3: Push to Back
Section 4 – Blocker Technique 4: Horizontal Strike to Head with Duck and Roundhouse Kick

18 *Ukemi* (Falling Techniques)   P. 163

Section 1 – *Ukemi* from Floor: Back Fall from Seated Position and Squat Position
Section 2 – *Ukemi* from Floor: Side Fall
Section 3 – *Ukemi* from Floor: Front Fall
Section 4 – *Ukemi* from Standing Position: Front Roll to Side Fall

19 Theory of Situational Self-defense   P. 169

Section 1 – The Grammar of Self-defense
Section 2 – *Kamae* (Posture)
Section 3 – *Kime*: Decisive, focused physical and mental power in execution of technique
Section 4 – *Ma-ai*: Correct distance
Section 5 – *Zan-shin*: The mind that remains to be alert
Section 6 – The Unwritten Self-defense Rule: "Get Away, Run Away, Right Away"

20 Basic Self-defense Techniques   P. 173

Section 1 – Cross-Single Wrist Grab with Anchor
Section 2 – Cross-Single Wrist Grab without Anchor
Section 3 – Straight-Single Wrist Grab without Anchor
Section 4 – Double-Wrist Grab Lower
Section 5 – Double-Wrist Grab Higher
Section 6 – Single-Wrist Grab by Two Hands
Section 7 – Two-Hand Choke or Grab from the Front to *Hiza-kuzushi*
Section 8 – Two-Hand Choke or Grab from Behind Escape Only
Section 9 – Two-Hand Choke or Grab from Behind to Outer Major Sweep
Section 10 – One-Arm (Bare-Arm) Choke from Behind
Section 11 – Bear Hug from Behind

21 Throws ~ Sweeps ~ Submissions   P. 191

Section 1 – Basic Wrist Throw (*Kote-nage*)
Section 2 – Shoulder Throw (*Seoi-nage*) from One-Arm Choke from Behind
Section 3 – Hip Throw (*Koshi-nage*)
Section 4 – Scissor Throw (*Hasami Nage*)
Section 5 – Outer Major Sweep (*O Soto-gari*)
Section 6 – Circular Block with Palm-Heel to Outer Major Sweep (*O Soto-gari*)
Section 7 – Double-Wrist Grab from Behind to *Kotenage*
Section 8 – Ground Arm-bar Submission (*Kansetsu-waza*)

22 Defense from the Ground or Seated Position   P. 207

Section 1 – Basic Posture for Ground Defense
 and How to Assume Basic Ground Defense Posture in Formal Practice
Section 2 – Ground Defense Against a Standing Attacker with Knee Attack (*Hiza-kizushi*)
Section 3 – Ground Defense Against a Choke
Section 4 – Defense from Seated Position: Basic Technique

Appendix and Bibliography   P. 215

Appendix – New York State Penal Code
Bibliography

WORKSHEETS

CHAPTER 1

Self-Defense in Context
A Historical Perspective of Non-violence and Self-defense

One, who overcomes by violence, will be overcome by violence.[1]

While the laws governing the right of self-defense vary from country to country, and more specifically within the United States, from state to state, one element of the self-defense law has been reasonably consistent for millennia—the law recognizes that the use of force in self-defense is a natural, innate response of human beings to protect themselves and/or their property from violent aggression; it's built into the human survival instinct.

Today, defensive techniques can be applied under the laws that protect the right of self-defense or defense of another (alter-ego defense). The law allows one "to use reasonable, defensive force against the aggressor who perpetrates the illegitimate attack, in order to repel this attack and to save a legitimate interest from the risk of injury…" including to defend one's life or the life of another.[2]

In addition to the confines of the law, this author adheres to a non-violent theory of self-defense. The theory of non-violent self-defense defines a strict ethical code to neutralize violence whenever possible by causing the least possible harm to the attacker, while fully protecting the would-be victim. In the practice of the art of self-defense, it is important to remember the non-violent principle as a guide to training; the highest aim in any self-defense situation is to stop the aggression, defuse conflict, while injuring no one.

A historical review of the world's major philosophical traditions reveals that there has been a dominant conviction that the right to self-defense rises from concepts in natural law[3]—the law of nature that identifies the action to defend one's self as inseparable from human nature. While "these traditions consider the person acting in self-defense to be morally right and justified... [none] considers the right to self-defense to be a boundless license to violence."[4]

---

[1] Laozi, Tzu, Lao. *Tao Te Ching*, translated by Arthur Waley, Wordsworth Editions Limited, 1997, p. 31.
[2] Sangero, Boaz. *Introduction. Self-Defence in Criminal Law* (Criminal Law Library; v. 1). N.p.: Hart Limited, 2006. p. 2. Print.
[3] Hessbruegge, Jan Arno. *Human Rights and Personal Self-Defense in International Law*. Oxford University Press, 2017. p. 30. eBook.
[4] Ibid.

In the West, specifically, the origins of moral and legal thought surrounding the right to self-defense within government are found in Greco-Roman traditions. Roman law considered "self-defense to be a natural right," which was "universally binding for both Romans and non-Romans." [5] However, at trial in a Roman court, it was incumbent on the defendant to persuade the jury that one's defensive action was reasonable, guided by defensive intent, and possibly further demonstrate necessity and proportionality of the defensive action, especially in defense of property.[6]

Julius Paulus, a distinguished Roman jurist, who served as praetorian prefect to the Roman Emperor, wrote in the second or third century CE "that all statutes and all rules of law allow people to repel force by force. [However, the law recognizes] clear limits of self-defense, namely that the force may only be directed against the aggressor and must have the object of self-defense and not revenge."[7]

Unlike ancient Western philosophical traditions, which looked to the law for the moral ground of the right for self-defense, ancient Asian cultures turned to oral traditions and religious or philosophical scriptures for guidance. For 2800 years, oral traditions and early writings in Asia agree that the practice of non-violence was essential to living a worthy life. In the fifth century BCE, Gautama Buddha taught the precepts of the Eightfold Path, one of which laid out the need for right action,[8] which included not killing or injuring. These teachings were later written in the *Tipitaka*, or *Pali Canon*, in the first century BCE. At the time, the Buddha's teaching of non-violence was not particularly connected to self-protection, but it was considered to be an essential virtue to achieve self-realization.

The first known written references to non-violence are found in Vedic texts, such as the *Chandogya Upanishad* (800-600 BCE), where non-violence (harmlessness) is listed as one of the five ethical observances which were practiced to express gratitude for receiving instruction from the enlightened souls.[9] The *Shandilya Upanishad* (100-300 BCE) is among the earliest texts to describe the eight-limb path of yoga, and it asserts that in order to walk this path of realization, one must begin by observing a high moral code based on self-control. This Upanishad outlines this moral code in the ten *yamas* (restraints) and the ten *niyamas* (observances). *Ahimsa*, a Sanskrit word meaning "not to injure or to harm, is identified as the first and most fundamental of the *yamas*.[10]

About the same time as the early Upanishads, the epic tale of the *Mahabharata* was first published in 300-400 BCE.[11] This text describes events over myriad generations and it holds possibly the first written philosophical discussions of justifications for breaking the promise of *ahimsa*. The argument in the *Mahabharata* is whether there is "just and moral ground" for the declaration of war on the

---

[5] Ibid. p. 31.
[6] Ibid.
[7] Ibid.
[8] Meyer, Milton Walter. *Asia: A Concise History*. Lanham, MD: Rowman & Littlefield, 1997. pp. 44-49 Print.
[9] Hume, Robert Ernest. The Thirteen Principal Upanishads: Translated from the Sanskrit with an Outline of the Philosophy of the Upanishads and an Annotated Bibliography, Oxford University Press, 1921, p. 213.
[10] Sastri, Alladi Mahadeva. *The Yoga-Upanishads*. Madras: Adyar Library, 1938. Print.
[11] Milman, Henry Hart, and Williams, Monier. *Story of Nala: An Episode of the Mahabharata*. Oxford: UP, 1860. p. xvii.

battlefield of Kurukshetra. The paradox within the debate is that the war was to be fought to stop the aggression of the Kaurava Clan to preserve the future of the Path of Righteousness (*Dharma*). Even though there is disagreement surrounding the details of the Mahabharata and the Kurukshetra War, such as the timeline, accuracy and even the existence of the event, few doubt the historical influence of the work as an allegory that highlights a profound and haunting dilemma—Is there such a thing as justifiable aggression? Are there circumstances in which the decision to wage war, while horrific, is not always the immoral choice? Today, thousands of years later, countries, religions and political groups remain locked in the ethical dialogue surrounding "a just war"—unsettled in what is a right position. As individuals, we find ourselves in a similar moral dilemma when witnessing an atrocity or confronted with the aggression of another.

About the same time as the first publishing of the *Mahabharata* in the fifth century BCE, in China, Sun Tzu's legendary text on military strategy, *Master Sun's Rules of War (The Art of War)* described how to achieve the most desired goal when confronted with military conflict. Much of Sun Tzu's treatise outlines how to fight without fighting, and how to use mental strategy to overcome the opponent without violence. Thomas Cleary's translation puts Master Sun's view succinctly, "A nation destroyed cannot be restored to existence and the dead cannot be restored to life ... to win without fighting is best." [12]

Even though Sun Tzu's work was written almost 2500 years ago and addresses the confrontation between states and nations, rather than the challenges of individual conflict, the heart of Sun Tzu's teaching has offered instructive wisdom for the student of self-defense (*ji-ei jutsu*) and the martial way *(budo)* for centuries. An example of this is vividly seen in an account of Tsukahara Bokuden (1489-1571), a master swordsman, who lived 2000 years after Sun Tzu.

The Tale of Bokuden on the following page illustrates *winning without fighting*.

---

[12] Sun Tzu, and Thomas F. Cleary. *The Art of War*. Boston, MA: Shambhala, 2005. 27. Print.

THE TALE OF BOKUDEN

Tsukahara Bokuden, one of the best-known warriors of sixteenth century Japan, used to travel with many followers. On one occasion he was traveling alone by boat. Although it was obvious that he was a samurai because of the two swords he carried, no one recognized that he was the legendary warrior. On the boat, there were many people from all walks of life, including merchants, craftsman, farmers, and a few samurai.

There was one particular samurai on the same boat, who spoke loudly and drew a great deal of attention to himself. He was busy bragging about his ability with the sword, claiming he was one of the best swordfighters in the country. People were afraid of him, so they pretended to show an interest in his story. But one person, who was sitting alone away from the others, did not seem to be interested in the samurai's story at all. It was Bokuden, who was minding his own business.

The samurai walked over to Bokuden and demanded his attention. But Bokuden continued to ignore him, which really irritated the samurai. At last, the samurai became so angry that he challenged Bokuden to a duel. But Bokuden refused to engage in sword fighting in such a crowded place, as innocent people could get hurt. The samurai agreed to wait until the boat reached the shore, and he ordered the boatman to the nearest island.

The samurai was already excited as he waited for the boat to arrive at the island. He swung his sword in front of people to loosen up for the combat. Bokuden was lying down, resting with his eyes closed. Finally, when the boat came close to the island, the bragging samurai shouted, "Come! You are now as good as dead. I will show you how sharp my sword is!" Bokuden did not reply but got up slowly. The samurai jumped off the boat and landed on the shore with the sword in his hands. As soon as the samurai stepped on the shore, Bokuden took the oar from the boatman and pushed the boat away from the shore. "You coward!" screamed the samurai, swinging his sword. Bokuden remained calm, smiled and declared, "This is called Victory without Fighting."

People on the boat laughed, watching the screaming samurai on the land. At the same time, they were impressed with Bokuden's tactics. Once they learned who Bokuden was, people bowed to him with reverence. *

> * Miyamoto, Musashi. A Way to Victory: The Annotated Book of Five Rings. Trans. and Commentary Hidy Ochiai. New York: Overlook, 2005. Pp 22-24. Print

Sun Tzu was not alone, however, in his contribution to defining peaceful means as the best reaction to aggression and violence. Between 600 and 100 BCE, the wisdom of many great philosophers and religious leaders was in harmony with Sun Tzu's view, such as Lao Tzu, Confucius, Gautama Buddha and Plato, who put forward doctrines which have continued to influence the thinking of humankind in this regard.

CHAPTER 2

Fighting Arts and Self-defense in Ancient History

Undoubtedly, skilled fighting and wrestling have been fundamental to human existence from prehistoric times. As an intrinsic part of cultures during the rise of civilization, fighting techniques and training became structured, and in time these skills were no longer used solely for defense, but also for ritual, sport and health.

Evidence of systematized fighting arts is clear in the earliest civilizations across the globe – Egypt, Mesopotamia, the Indus Valley and Indian sub-continent, Huang-He (Yellow) River Valley, Southeast Asia, Anatolia Plateau (Asia Minor), the Mediterranean and the Americas. While the origins of many of these arts and their relationship to each other remain murky, since many claim roots in myth, what has been documented from the writings, sculpture, carvings and drawings of the ancient civilizations is certain evidence of fist-striking matches, grappling, throwing and submission techniques, sometimes combined with stick-fighting and often with participants wearing a rope, cloth or leather belt.

To illustrate fighting arts in antiquity, the following is a brief discussion of belt-wrestling and stick-fighting in Ancient Egypt.

ANCIENT EGYPT (THE NILE RIVER VALLEY)

Ancient Egypt is one of the most studied ancient civilizations. The extensive knowledge we have of life in ancient Egypt arises not only from the volume of well-documented images and artifacts, but also from the good fortune of finding a piece of stone from an ancient stela (pillar) in the port city of Rosetta in 1799 (top left of map). The Rosetta Stone was engraved with three versions of the same decree written in 196 BCE. The first two were in ancient Egyptian scripts (the older Hieroglyphic script and the newer Demotic script) and the third script was Ancient Greek, which enabled archaeologists to understand the two Egyptian scripts.

About 3200 BCE, Egypt comes out of the prehistoric age and into the Early Dynastic Period with the rise of the first Pharaoh, Narmer, who unified Upper and Lower Egypt and established the first "states" along the Nile River.[13] This timing roughly coincides with the rise of civilizations in Mesopotamia.

During this period, the city of Aswan, at the First Cataract (an area of shallow water on the Nile), marked the southern border of Egypt. Beyond it lay Nubia (now known as Sudan) and a culture of the indigenous people who lived further south along the Nile (lower right of map). Aswan was a point of trade between Ancient Egyptian monarchs and Nubia.[14]

The people of Nubia were known to be skilled in wrestling and stick-fighting and were often depicted in drawings in caves of Ancient Egypt. The cultural interaction between Egypt and Nubia contributed to the early development of this region's fighting arts.

---

[13] Wilkinson, Toby A. H. *Early Dynastic Egypt*, Routledge, 2005, pp. 56-57.

[14] Carroll, Scott T.: "Wrestling in Ancient Nubia", Journal of Sport History, Vol. 15, No. 2 (Summer, 1988)

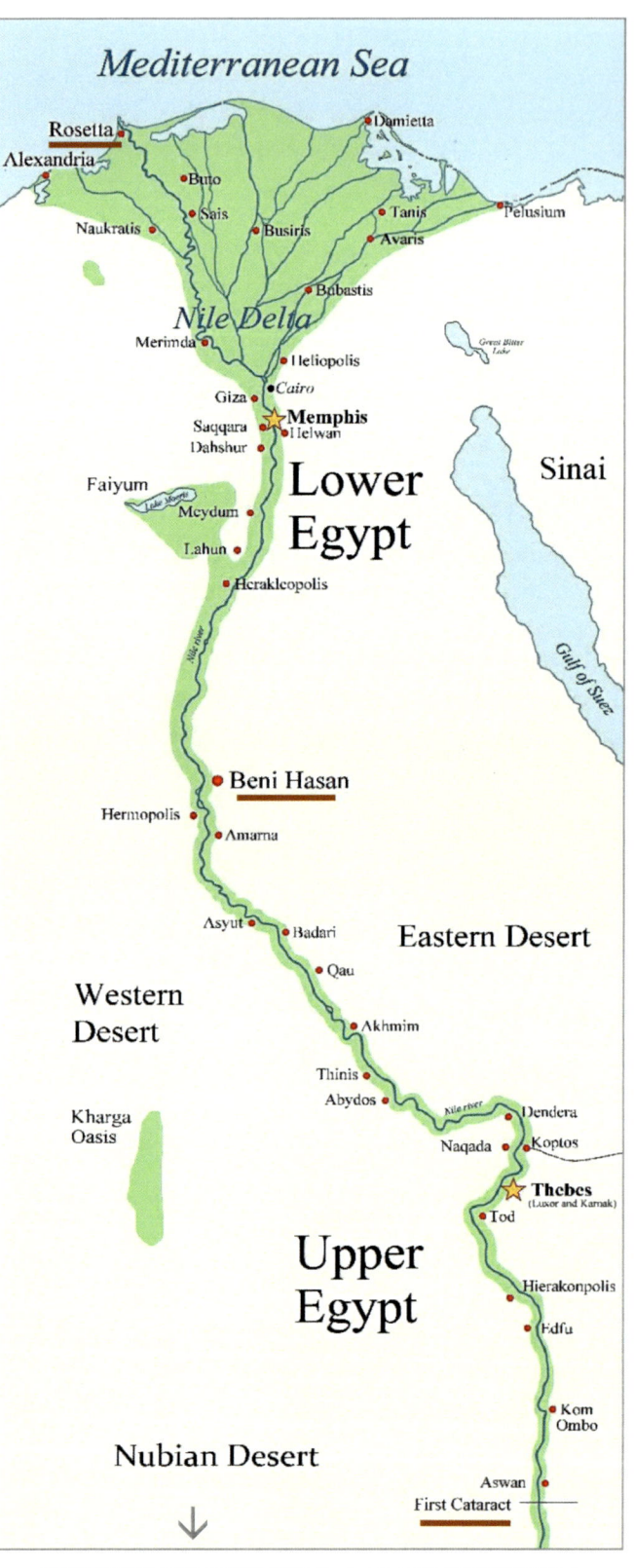

MAP OF EGYPT: Jeff Dahl [GFDL (http://www.gnu.org/copyleft/fdl.html) or CC BY-SA 4.0 https://creativecommons.org/licenses/by-sa/4.0)], via Wikimedia Commons Wrestling at the tombs of Beni Hassan

"Evidence regarding ancient Nubian wrestling is derived from Egyptian archaeological sources and a literary reference in Heliodorus' *Aethiopica*. A careful anthropological investigation of the modern Sudanese tribes reveals a wrestling culture thriving among the Nuba people. African wrestling champions [were brought] from their villages to wrestle in the Pharaoh's tribute games. The ancient Nubian tradition [of wrestling] is still practiced fervently [today]." [15]

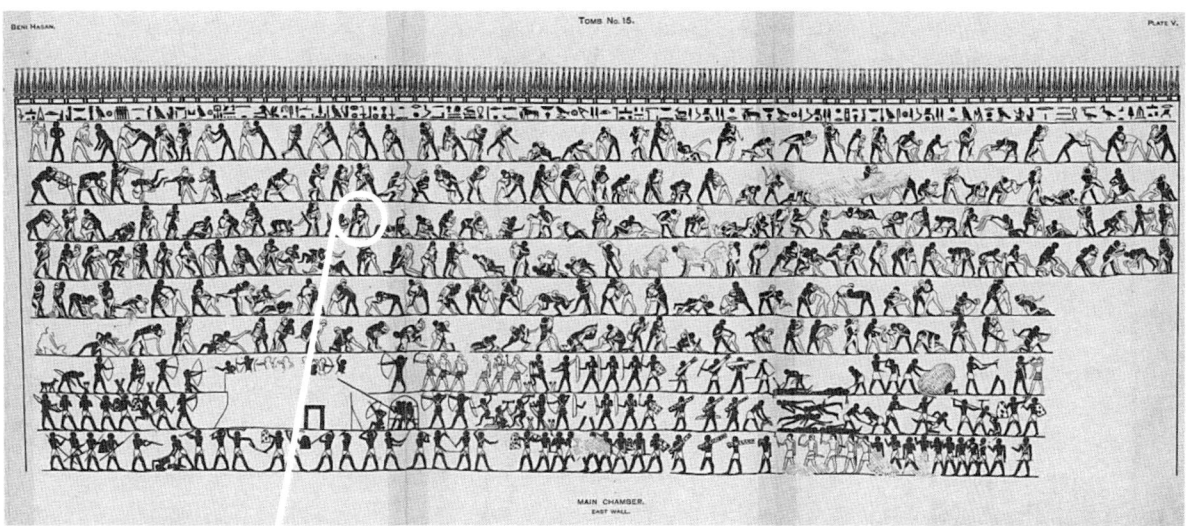

TOP: Beni Hasan Tomb 15 – Main Chamber East Wall (plate v.) [16]
LEFT: Enlarged Image from massive Main Chamber (plate iii.) [17]

Sir John Gardner Wilkinson (1797–1875) was a traveler, writer and pioneer Egyptologist who wrote in 1874: "The grottoes of Beni Hassan show wrestling was a favourite amusement; and the paintings present all the varied attitudes and modes of attack and defence of which it is susceptible. And, in order to enable the spectator more readily to perceive the position of the limbs of each combatant, the artist [who painted the walls of the tombs] has availed himself…to introduce alternately a black and red figure." [18]

In this case (left), the red figure in the front is reacting to the hold across his upper torso by executing a inner major hook throw, known as *O Uchi Gake*.

---

[15] Ibid.
[16] "Newberry, Percy E.: Beni Hasan (Band 2) (London, 1893)."Vereinigung Bildender Künstler Österreichs Secession [Hrsg.]: Ver Sacrum: Mittheilungen Der Vereinigung Bildender Künstler Österreichs (1.1898), University of Heidelberg, 2012, digi.ub.uni-heidelberg.de/diglit/newberry1893bd2/0105/image.
[17] Ibid.
[18] Wilkinson, John Gardner. *A Popular Account of the Ancient Egyptians. from His Larger Work*, by Sir J. Gardner Wilkinson. Illustrated with Five Hundred Woodcuts. Vol. 1, J. Murray, 1874. pp.204-205.

As was the case with wrestling in the ancient world, stick-fighting gradually became a ritualized art that was performed at festivals in honor of the Gods. In Ancient Egypt, this sparring with sticks in time drew an Arabic name, *al-tahtib* or *tahtib*.[19]

Stick-fighting from Beni Hasan Tomb 15 (Close up of image on previous page—plate v.)

Tahtib is a spontaneously organized match in which two men swirl long wooden or bamboo staffs, while leaping and circling an opponent in attempt to strike the other with "a deft numbing blow. This is a contest of skill, based on balance, agility and muscle control rather than brute strength… As one admits defeat, another spectator rises to challenge the victor."[20]

A NOTE ABOUT ORIGINS OF FIGHTING ARTS IN EAST ASIA & FINDING TRUTH IN ANTIQUITY

The history of fighting arts in antiquity is a vast and understudied topic. In modern history, few regions have seen the breadth of systemization of fighting skills as much as East Asia, and as a result considerable effort has been made to piece together the facts in this region. In 1997 a book titled, *Chinese Martial Arts History* by Guojia Tiwei Wushu Yanjiu Yuan, et. al, was published, and a review of the text declared: "[This work] is the first official historical survey of the martial arts ever published for general distribution in China. Thus, by its very existence, it represents a new era in study and interpretation in the field…The subject has rarely been discussed in the past outside a small circle, even in the Chinese physical culture and sports community, not to mention outside China."[21]

Since this 1997 ground-breaking publication, Cambridge University released a highly researched, scholarly text in 2012 by Dr. Peter Lorge, *Chinese Martial Arts: From Antiquity to the Twenty-first Century*. Dr. Lorge sought to rectify many inaccurate assumptions, which had become "history" during the last century. Also, Shoshin Nagamine's several books on Okinawan martial arts and Patrick McCarthy's work, *Bubishi: Bible of Karate*, have tried assiduously to correct errors about the evolution of martial arts in the Ryukyu Kingdom—now Okinawa.

Today, the actual origins of fighting arts in East Asia continue to be uncovered. In time, their roots may be found in the ancient cultures of India's Indus-Ganga plain, which developed the earliest system of medicine, outlined energy fields of the body and created exercises/postures to promote health and self-mastery. Or, their origins may be discovered in the ancient southern kingdoms of

---

[19] Wickett, Elizabeth. "Archaeological Memory, the Leitmotifs of Ancient Egyptian Festival Tradition, and Cultural Legacy in the Festival Tradition of Luxor: the Mulid of Sidi Abu'l Hajjaj Al-Uqsori and the Ancient Egyptian 'Feast of Opet.'" Journal of the American Research Center in Egypt, vol. 45, 2009, pp. 403–426. JSTOR, JSTOR, www.jstor.org/stable/25735464. Page 416

[20] Ibid.

[21] Henning, Stanley E. "China Review International." China Review International, vol. 5, no. 2, 1998, pp. 417–424. JSTOR, JSTOR, www.jstor.org/stable/23732360.

India, a region called Tamilakam—now known as Tamil Nadu, Kerala, southern Andhra Pradesh, parts of Karnataka and northern Sri Lanka. The seaports of ancient Tamilakam were hubs of commerce between Rome and China beginning in the first century CE, and the people of Tamilakam had developed advanced systemized fighting arts, which are referenced in ancient Tamil literature written hundreds of years earlier. This highlights an important point: Without a correct understanding of human mobility and cultural interchange in ancient times, it is impossible to know how art forms, such as fighting skills, truly evolved.

Currently, many historical texts agree that essential cultural exchange of arts began in about 200-300 BCE at trade centers along the land and maritime routes of the Silk Roads, which eventually stretched from far eastern points of Asia to the western Mediterranean. However, the use of technological innovation is staged to upend this current historical view.

One such case: In 2017, an archaeological team from Washington University in St. Louis used satellite imagery, GIS and human geography to discover a vast network of east-west trade pathways in the mountainous region of the Silk Roads, which originated from the seasonal herding trails formed by nomads 5,000 years ago.[22] The flow of these trails "form a near-continuous geography of 'pathways' that discreetly connect over 74% of the highland Silk Road sites [at elevations of] 750 meters to 4000 meters."[23] Further, this research revealed that exchange between nomadic herding communities and their neighbors resulted in sophisticated and widespread "distribution of commodities, technologies and ideologies already by 2500 BC along the inner Asian mountain corridor… [This] exchange of cultural practices occurred in the Bronze Age *without* the driving force of state-structured political authorities."[24]

In a sense, finding truth in antiquity is an ever-receding goal. As the quest to understand life in ancient civilizations will require an increasingly broad range of scientific disciplines to assimilate each other's data, it may be valuable to remember Socrates' words.

> *Now, therefore, with careful thought and due consideration, paying attention neither to the usefulness nor to the reputation of any arts or sciences, but to that faculty [inherent power] of our souls, if such there be, which by its nature loves the truth and does all things for the sake of the truth, let us examine this faculty.*[25]
>
> (*Philebus* by Plato)

If one accepts that it is the nature of a human being to love the truth, then it is *that part* of ourselves that deserves our respect, attention and humility.

---

[22] Frachetti, Michael D., et al. "Nomadic Ecology Shaped the Highland Geography of Asia's Silk Roads." Nature News, Nature Publishing Group, 8 Mar. 2017, www.nature.com/articles/nature21696. pp. 195-196.
[23] Ibid.
[24] Ibid.
[25] Plato. *Plato in Twelve Volumes, Vol. 9* translated by Harold N. Fowler. Cambridge, MA, Harvard University Press; London, William Heinemann Ltd. 1925. The Annenberg CPB/Project
http://www.perseus.tufts.edu/hopper/text?doc=Perseus%3Atext%3A1999.01.0174%3Atext%3DPhileb.%3Asection%3D58d

CHAPTER 3

Ji-ei Jitsu (Self-Defense) ~ *To-Te* (Chinese Hand) ~ *Dō* (The Way)

Section 1 - The Ryukyu Kingdom: Self-Defense and Non-Violence

Directly and indirectly, the theory of self-defense has been linked to the moral principle of non-violence for hundreds of years. Historically, the development of self-defense arts, and particularly *Te* (hand), primarily took place in the Ryukyu Kingdom (Okinawa), a small archipelago on a line between the East China Sea and the Pacific Ocean. *Te*, in the Okinawan language, was an indigenous martial art practiced mainly by the nobility on the island.

As was the case with so many historic advances in civilization, geography played a key role. The islands of the Ryukyu Kingdom were a pathway of stepping stones that linked trade between East Asia and Southeast Asia. For almost 600 years (13th to 19th centuries), the Ryukyu Islands were not only a hub of commerce and culture in Asia, they were a meeting place of exchange of techniques of self-defense arts, particularly with travelers to and from China and Japan.

In the preface of the *Bubishi*, by Patrick McCarthy, Mr. Li Yiduan, Deputy Secretary General of the Fuzhou Branch of All China Athletic Federation, stated:

> "The cultural heritage of China had for centuries profoundly influenced those societies with which it once traded. Among those cultures most affected by the 'Middle Kingdom' was the Ryukyu archipelago, and in particular the people of Okinawa.
>
> Based on the remnants of an ancient grappling discipline cultivated in Okinawa [*Te*]…and combined with the principles of Chinese *gongfu*, which had been continuously introduced to the archipelago from before recorded history, a number of indigenous self-defense methods gradually developed."

Three primary styles of *Te* developed in Okinawa: *Shuri-te* and *Naha-te* and *Tomari-te*. Each style is named for the town in Okinawa in which it originated. In addition to *Te*, which consisted of techniques that were more strictly of Okinawan origin, there was also such a fighting style known as *To-te* in Okinawa. *To-te* (in this context, literally, "Chinese hand") was an indigenous fighting system that had been influenced more directly by the elements of Chinese empty-hand fighting techniques.

It should be noted, however, that some people have held the notion that *To-te* and *Te* are actually the same thing, and some used the expression *To-te* to impress others, since there was a general tendency at that time to regard anything Chinese as more noble and respectable. (The word "*To*" comes from the name of a once prosperous Chinese dynasty, and it was used to denote "China.") Strictly speaking, however, it may be appropriate to distinguish *Te* from *To-te*.

A NON-VIOLENT PHILOSPHY MERGES WITH JI-EI JITSU

The ancient edict of non-violence, as it developed in Japan within the art of self-defense, was well expressed by a famous Japanese Zen Buddhist priest, Muso Soseki, who lived in the thirteenth century. Shoshin Nagamine highlights the story in his text: "One day during a boat voyage, the priest Muso was attacked by a thug who split his head open with an oar. Caught off-guard, the *deshi* (disciple) of Muso immediately lunged to fight in retaliation. However, Muso restrained his *deshi* and chanted these words, 'The attacker and the defender are both nothing more than part of an incident in an illusion which exists but for only a moment in the span of one's life.' "[26]

While Soseki's profound declaration is far beyond ordinary understanding, it reveals the early influence of Zen in the Japanese art of *ji-ei jutsu* (self-defense). *Ji-ei jutsu*, at its highest level, rests on knowing the True Self. Master Soseki's response arises from an enlightened mind—seeing the self and others as one, and the self and nature as one. A mind, with less developed awareness, mistakenly identifies the self only as separate and distinct from others. This limited view of reality is a source of disharmony and thus inevitably leads to perpetual conflict. When the self is not perceived as separate from others, there is no conflict.

Other than the possible overall influence of Buddhist monks and Bodhidharma from India in the sixth and seventh centuries in Shaoshi region of China,[27] historically the merger of self-defense arts with Zen and non-violent philosophy primarily took place in Japan. Two masters influenced the synthesis of Zen and self-defense through discussions of the principles of sword fighting. The first, Takuan Soho (1573-1645) was a renowned priest in the Rinzai sect of Zen Buddhism and the second, Miyamoto Musashi (1584-1645) was a legendary swordsman. Takuan said about sword fighting "…when the heart is troubled no more by thought of I and You, of the opponent and his sword, of one's own sword and how to wield it—no more thought even of life and death, there is no time lag between evasion and action. It is as if the sword wields itself."[28] Such a mind flows readily, without hesitation, relaxed yet fully aware, and it burns off the impulse to initiate violence and seeks only to restore peace.

---

[26] Nagamine, Shoshin. Trans. Patrick McCarthy. *Tales of Okinawa's Great Masters*. Boston: Tuttle Pub., 2000. p. 23. Print.

[27] Lorge, Peter Allan. *Chinese Martial Arts: from Antiquity to the Twenty-First Century*. Cambridge University Press, pp. 105-108. 2012.
NOTE: While Lorge maintains that there is little evidence to link Bodhidharma to the origins of marital arts in China, it is reasonable to consider that the highly educated Brahmin monks from India might have influenced training regimens of monks in China and Japan in the early centuries CE, particularly given that the ports of India were a hub of commerce between the Rome and China beginning in the first century CE.

[28] Herrigel, Eugen. *Zen*. New York: McGraw-Hill, 1964. P. 104. Print.

Musashi's life was dedicated to achieving the highest level of skill as a swordsman for self-defense. His renowned treatise on swordsmanship, *The Book of Five Rings*, outlines the importance of constant, mental and physical training, so one can attain true peace within and peace with others. The first four volumes of the *Five Rings* solely focus on martial strategy and fighting techniques. The fifth and final volume, titled *Ku* states, "*Ku* is the realm of matters beyond human understanding. ...As long as one is not enlightened about the Way of Truth, one might believe that one's own Way is correct. ...It could happen, however, that [one's way] will not be in accordance with the Truth...[as it] is possible to unconsciously ignore the true Way simply by being self-centered or prejudiced. One must understand this point well." [29]

In this volume, Musashi echoes Soseki and Takuan stating that in order to achieve true non-violence, one's mind and spirit must reside in oneness. "In a concrete sense, *Ku* is the domain of an enlightened individual who has reached the highest stage of his art. One becomes harmonious with the universe. The fact that Musashi experienced more than sixty life-and-death battles makes his insight truly authentic... His world of *Ku* is where total peacefulness prevails—there is no killing or fighting...there."[30]

Given the above illustrations of an enlightened mind, traditional students of self-defense may incorporate sitting quietly in *mokuso* to practice breathing and awareness—to gradually gain mastery of one's heart/mind (*kokoro*). This practice enables one to unify the mind, technique and body (*shin-gi-tai*). When this oneness, or unification, has been achieved, one becomes a true *katsujin ken* (a person whose sword gives life)—one who is able to win without fighting. For more on *mokuso*, see Chapter 7: *The Breath, Energy and Ki-ai*.

"DŌ" (THE WAY): SELF-DEFENSE AS AN ART

Particularly in Asia, within the past 500 years and with the influence of Zen, ancient forms of self-defense grew into martial arts training systems. These martial arts became a physical metaphor for a path to live a virtuous and harmonious life.

After centuries of war in Feudal Japan (1185-1603), the Tokugawa Shogunate (1603-1868) established a prosperous and peaceful time for the Japanese. With peace across the nation, the samurai culture placed a greater emphasis on self-cultivation through fine arts, meditation and introspection, all found in Zen Buddhist philosophy. Zen priests viewed the warriors' intense ascetic training as similar to Zen meditation and as a means to overcome the delusions of the ego. In the Tokugawa Shogunate, the samurai became a symbolic source of stability for society, as they practiced their fighting skills more as an art, than for combat.

Today, traditional Japanese martial arts – *budo* (martial way) – continue to cultivate a way of life that encompasses physical, spiritual and moral dimensions focused on self-improvement.

---

[29] Miyamoto, Musashi. *A Way to Victory: The Annotated Book of Five Rings*. Trans. Hidy Ochiai. New York: Overlook, 2005. 143. Print.
[30] Ibid, p. 145

Throughout the world, in traditional training halls of martial arts (*dojo*), the practitioner of martial arts (*budoka*) is taught ideals that originated in samurai culture. In Japan, the Nippon Budokan was established in 1964 to preserve the teaching of self-cultivation through *budo*.[31]

A modern master of traditional martial arts, Gichin Funakoshi, popularized the phrase *Karate ni sente nashi*. "Literally translated *karate ni sente nashi* says 'fist that does not strike first' … [However] A deeper extension of the translation is 'the fists that give life.'"[32] This means that one should never make the first offensive move or provoke violence. The principle of not initiating violence is not meant to convey mere passivity, however, because in a life and death struggle, a good offense could be the best defense.

Karate ni sente nashi means that preventing dangerous or violent situations is most desirable in the art of self-defense. Prevention may include leaving the danger, deflecting the attack, or not responding at all. Many individuals have saved their own lives by not reacting aggressively to an assault. However, since timing is often critical to successfully securing safety, one must develop awareness to ascertain how best to secure peace.

Interestingly, there is another important saying in martial arts that is seemingly contradictory to the above-mentioned teaching, *Karate wa sente nari*, which is literally translated as "Karate is the first move." This implies that one must be ahead of others in action at all times in order to suppress violence. Of course, this teaching does not only concern a pre-emptive physical action, but it also conveys the importance of psychological insight and tactics in mental self-defense.

Understanding the true meaning of the two apparently different tenets reveals that there is no contradiction between them. In essence, they teach us to never use physical strength and techniques acquired through training, except in a case of absolute self-defense. At the same time, these tenets remind us to remain alert, so we can thwart potential danger.

> *The true student of the art of self-defense seeks harmony among people.*
> *The highest aim in any self-defense situation is to stop the aggression, defuse conflict, while injuring no one.*

---

[31] "FAQ." ENGLISH GUIDE, Nippon Budokan, 2016, www.nipponbudokan.or.jp/english.
[32] Nagamine, Shoshin. Trans. Patrick McCarthy. *Tales of Okinawa's Great Masters*. Boston: Tuttle Pub., 2000. p. 163

Section 2 - Definition of Non-Violence and the Choice of Peace for the Individual

One would think that humanity has enough problems coping with natural disasters such as earthquakes, typhoons, fires and floods. However, the magnitude of the suffering due to natural catastrophes pales in comparison to suffering caused by human acts of violence. Throughout history, violence has taken a tremendous toll on humanity. Individuals, communities and countries are scarred by the impact of violence, and it can take generations for healing to take hold.

For society, the task of reducing violence may be best addressed at the grass-roots level— through the education of children. If children learn early that hatred and violence are destructive to their own lives, as well as to the lives of others, a desire to find peaceful resolutions will guide their decisions in adulthood.

To educate children toward the "choice of peace," an important first step is to emphasize a sound definition of non-violence. The term "non-violence" often applies to a non-aggressive method of achieving social or political change, such as Mahatma Gandhi's use of non-violent, civil disobedience to overthrow British rule to achieve political independence for India. In the context of this text, however, non-violence is applied as a protocol for the resolution of conflict between individuals.

While obviously a moral code of non-violence would include the pre-requisite of non-aggression, what is a less obvious characteristic of non-violence is the need to stop violence when it occurs. If the goal is peace, then a more complete definition of non-violence would be: "Don't act with violence toward others and don't become a victim of violence." For one not to become a victim, one must defensively stop violence with minimal harm.

It is a well-known fact that the human being's primal response to a real or perceived threat is the fight-or-flight reaction. This reaction occurs involuntarily. With proper guidance and training, one can use self-awareness, intellect and self-control to harness the natural energy of the fight-or-flight response to resolve potentially violent situations as safely as possible. The cultivation of this degree of self-mastery is the principal objective of self-defense training.

Therefore, in the education of individuals, and particularly children, there must be a sound self-defense training program, which engages the entirety of the individual—body, mind and heart, so as to achieve heightened levels of self-control and a deep understanding for the need for civility. With consistent training, children will develop the respect, confidence and self-discipline needed to find more peace within themselves. Additionally, they will gain skill in defensive techniques, so they will be less likely to be victims of violence. Under a capable teacher, the most broken-spirited, confused and violence-prone young adults and children can become less spiteful, more confident and more productive in life.

Section 3 – Distinction between Self-Defense and Martial Arts

Effective self-defense techniques have been developed and polished by highly skilled practitioners over the centuries and most have their roots in ancient forms of martial arts. However, in real-life, any method that is effective in protecting one's life is self-defense. In this sense, self-defense techniques are fundamentally instinctive and based on common sense, not formalized martial arts techniques.

While it goes without saying that correct technical methods of self-defense are critically important, it must also be emphasized that in a life-or-death struggle, mental strength and willpower can prove to be more important than physical technique. Sound judgment and ingenuity can often create a vital window of opportunity for escape or to gain control of dangerous circumstances. For example, striking the face of an attacker with a backpack or jabbing the side of an attacker's rib cage with a set of keys could be a life-saving technique in self-defense. Theoretically, neither of these escape methods is part of systematized self-defense training or traditional martial arts.

Ultimately, the purpose of self-defense training is to strengthen oneself physically and mentally, so that when a real situation arises, one can respond effectively. *Practice as if it's real, so when it's real, it will be like practice.*

True self-defense training at its highest level must include the individual's total development—physical, mental, and spiritual. After all, it is the "totality of the self" that executes the defense that might save one's life.

CHAPTER 4

The Study of Self-Defense and Individual Development

The art of self-defense may be in a category of its own among the physical arts because it holds a key to cultivating stronger and more confident individuals who seek to take control and responsibility for their life and are not afraid to pursue their dreams. The practice of self-defense constantly reinforces one's self-respect and place in the world—silently expressing the message, "I am worth defending. My life is valuable."

> *Studying the art of self-defense inspires one to work gradually toward becoming the "master of the self" and to live a life of intention and meaning.*

It is the author's philosophy that one's life offers both an opportunity, as well as a responsibility, to make the most of it. Appreciation for life can be expressed by committing oneself to self-development — "to be the best that one can be." In this way, each person becomes a steward of his or her own life. The study and practice of self-defense inspires one to remain true to one's self and to one's purpose.

Section 1 – The Mind-Body Connection Theory: The Heart of Self-Defense Training

It is the author's experience that no student can become truly proficient in the art of self-defense without strengthening the mind-body connection. Protecting oneself requires the entire being to be engaged harmoniously. When there is little or no time to think, the body must respond instantly to the mind's perception of danger. Focused training over a long period of time will help one to internalize self-defense techniques, so that the body will respond instinctively from muscle memory. Undue hesitation can be the difference between life and death. In most cases, the initial impulse to implement self-defense occurs in the flash of a moment. The first and best choice is to get away from danger as quickly as possible.

Therefore, a sound theory of self-defense must define the method by which one can develop the clear-sightedness and willpower to prevail in a vast number of potentially threatening situations. An important tenet of this author's approach to traditional self-defense training is that physiology creates psychology. It is through the refinement of physical techniques in a prescribed, purposeful manner that the individual's mind and character are transformed. The reverse of this is also true. Psychology creates physiology. In a self-defense situation, the mind instinctively will lead the body. However, for the mind to lead the body correctly, it must be strong, aware and disciplined to adapt and to make good decisions. For example, distancing oneself from reckless individuals—such as not getting in a car with a friend who has had too much to drink, even if this is a ride home—is sound self-defense. Although it may be inconvenient and cause momentary hurt feelings, the higher good is not to risk one's life or the lives of others.

Another commonplace circumstance which requires a disciplined mind is not to escalate a conflict with someone who is provoking a fight. This situation can go from bad to worse very quickly even resulting in a life-threatening situation. The difficulty with applying common sense to diffuse a heated turn-of-events is that it often requires one to give way. In recent years, road-rage incidents have tragically ended in serious, even deadly, confrontations, because drivers won't let go of feeling infuriated by another's actions. At times, one's inner strength must demonstrate humble, forgiving and self-effacing behavior to make the wise and safest choice. It is important to remember that children learn how to handle interactions with people and the world at a young age through example and training (see Chapter 4, Section 3: Definition of a "Strong Person").

The following writing by Laozi speaks of the profound effectiveness of yielding.

> *There is nothing under Heaven as soft and pliant as water; Yet in striking against the hard and rigid,*
> *There is nothing more capable of success.*
> *This being as it is, there is nothing that could easily take its place.*
>
> *The pliant defeats the rigid; The soft defeats the hard.*[33]

---

[33] Laozi, and William Scott Wilson. *Tao Te Ching: An All-New Translation*, Shambhala, 2013, p. 141.

Therefore, being mindful of one's thoughts, emotions and physical potential will enable one to attain a vital skill—the ability to do what one intends to do. Phrases such as "My emotions ran away with me," or "I don't know what I was thinking when I did that," are often the remorseful cry after a tragic event. Without the self-control that comes from harmonization of the mind and body, proficiency in self-defense is impossible.

Below is an interesting story from ancient times that illustrates the remarkable physical skill, which can emanate from a unified mind and absolute belief in the self.

BELIEF AND CONFIDENCE: A MUSASHI ANECDOTE

It was in the late afternoon of a midsummer day. After traveling all day, Miyamoto Musashi was resting at a small mountain inn, enjoying the scenery as well as a cup of tea. The place was part of Harima province (the present Hyogo prefecture). Musashi's tranquil moment was interrupted when a strange boy approached him. The boy looked very serious. He bowed down deeply to Musashi and started to speak, "Miyamoto Sensei (teacher or master). My father was recently killed by a samurai who used a very dishonorable method, and I, as the oldest son of the family, must avenge his death." As he spoke, the boy became even more serious and his voice, trembling, sounded determined to enter a life-or-death combat.

"So, you want me to help you fight your opponent who killed your father, right?" Musashi asked the boy gently, expecting that the boy should be allowed to have some help in the duel against a samurai. But, surprisingly, the boy shook his head and rejected Musashi's offer, declaring, "I am only thirteen years old and I know I am not strong enough yet to fight a real samurai on an equal basis. But it is my duty to fight him and, if possible, defeat my opponent with my own hands so that my father's soul can rest peacefully in heaven." Musashi was impressed by the boy's proper attitude and strong spirit. It was obvious to Musashi that the boy came from a proud samurai family, for he conducted himself, despite his young age, with a dignity and self-discipline that were becoming of a would-be samurai.

"Miyamoto Sensei, I have heard about you from many people. Even my father, while alive, used to speak of you as the greatest warrior in this land." As the boy spoke, his eyes became larger, gradually showing a boyish feature in his manner; he was finally feeling the excitement of meeting the legendary warrior. "Sir, if I may, I have one very important request, if I may. Would you please teach me a technique that will make me able to defeat my opponent in this coming duel? I do not fear death, but I want to make sure that I can kill my opponent, no matter what. Is it possible, sir?"

Musashi silently observed the boy's face for a while and he was impressed by the earnest attitude of the young samurai; so, he decided to help him. "All right, young man. Listen to me carefully. I will now give you one very special technique that will make you the victor in the coming duel." Musashi's voice was slow and deliberate. The boy immediately sat down in front of Musashi, in a formal manner, with his eyes intently fixed on Musashi's face.

"Now, this is what you must do. When you meet your opponent, hold the short sword in your left hand and the regular one in your right hand. Carry both swords high above your shoulders as you advance toward your opponent. When the distance between you and your opponent becomes close, stand still and wait for him to attack you first. Your opponent will try to stab you in the chest, at which moment you must quickly parry his attack with your sword in the right hand and with all your might, thrust out your short sword in the left hand against your opponent's chest. You must do it as if you are stabbing him through to his back." Musashi stopped here for a few moments and observed the boy with a stern face, but his compassion for the boy was obvious as he continued to talk.

"No matter what happens don't hesitate to block and attack for there is no question that you will be victorious. This technique will work for you without doubt." The boy listened to Musashi with total concentration and soon he stood up. He took a short sword in his left hand and the regular sword in the right, as told. It was not easy for the boy to hold the regular sword in one hand, but he tried his best to follow Musashi's instructions.

"Miyamoto Sensei, is this the correct way?" The boy sought Musashi's approval as he wielded the swords repeatedly. The boy was very determined and demonstrated more power and skill than any other thirteen-year-old boy could. "Very good, young man. Very good!" Musashi's heavy voice praised the boy, who was encouraged to continue the same motions many times. After a while, Musashi stopped the boy's practice and said, "Young man, I have one more thing to share with you for your absolute victory in the duel."

"Yes, sir." The boy immediately positioned himself in the formal sitting posture and looked anxiously toward Musashi.

"Now, I know that you will be able to avenge your father's death, without doubt, by using the technique that I have just taught you." Musashi stressed the boy's would-be victory, after which he became silent. He slowly moved his eyes to the sky, which was getting dark, but still one could see a brilliant red color over the mountains far away. Was it that Musashi was reminiscing about his first duel when he killed Arima Kihei? Musashi, then called Ben-no-suke, had been thirteen years old at that time, the same age as the boy.

Musashi looked down at the boy again and, in a mysterious tone, started to speak. "There is no question that you are going to win this battle. But you are still young and your opponent is an experienced samurai. I think it is good if I give you an additional power that will make you certain of your victory. That is, I am going to pray to the God of Ants, who will protect you against your opponent for sure. You stand facing your opponent, just before you advance toward him, remember to look down at the ground where you stand.

If an ant is found crawling around near your feet, it means that the God of Ants has listened to my prayer and in no way can you lose." So, saying, Musashi closed his eyes and started to pray, pressing his palms together. The boy watched Musashi and followed the gesture of praying.

It is important to note that Musashi directly mentions in one of his writings, Dokko-Do (The Path of Lone Walk), "I respect Buddha and gods, but I do not depend on them," which highlights Musashi's absolute belief in self-power, ji-riki. Therefore, whatever he was doing for the sake of the boy's situation, Musashi's gesture of praying to the God of Ants was not religious in nature. Rather it was a gesture to induce a certain psychological strength in the young samurai.

In any event, on the day of the duel, the boy dressed in a colorful costume with a white headband. His father would have been very proud of him. As he walked to the site of the duel, the boy's face was full of concentration and determination. He saw his opponent in the distance. The boy stopped to draw the two swords, as instructed by Musashi. He raised both swords high above his shoulders and was then ready to advance toward the opponent. He then remembered, as Musashi had told him, to look down at the ground where he stood, hoping to find an ant as the sure sign of his victory. It was the middle of summer. You couldn't miss an ant on the ground, no matter where you looked. Not only one or two, but hundreds of small ants were crawling all around his feet. The boy became even more confident of his victory, believing that the God of Ants was on his side, as Musashi had prayed on his behalf.

The boy walked toward his opponent with a confident manner and with his eyes focused on the opponent at all times. As predicted by Musashi, the opponent thrust out the sword to stab the boy in the chest. The boy blocked it with the sword in his right hand and counter-attacked with the short sword in his left hand. The boy won, successfully avenging his father's death and thus restoring honor to his family.

As this anecdote indicates, Musashi's greatness lies not only in the fact that he was an extraordinary fighting strategist, but also that he was a psychologist of sorts. Musashi used a psychological technique to get the boy to believe in himself and absolute victory, which resulted in the defeat of a samurai by a mere thirteen-year-old boy. If we ignore the social background in which Musashi had to survive, it is easy to be misled into thinking of him as a ruthless, cunning character. But, as we can appreciate from this story, he was compassionate as well. His intelligence was also noteworthy, especially for a samurai of that era. It is now known that psychology, properly administered, is a powerful tool in accomplishing many things. Musashi was already familiar with this mental strategy in his time and used it to induce an almost miraculous inner strength in the boy by "psyching him up." Musashi himself must have used the same technique to encourage himself and to survive more than sixty combats, all of which he won.*

---

* Miyamoto, Musashi. A Way to Victory: The Annotated Book of Five Rings. Trans. Hidy Ochiai. New York: Overlook, pp.143. 18-21. Print.

Section 2 – The Upward Spiral: Development of Positive Character Traits through Self-Defense Training

The required mind/body integration found in traditional self-defense training offers a holistic mechanism for the development of positive character traits in the individual, as if to offer a framework, which reflects one's progress. While the specifics of how each student develops varies considerably, there are certain guideposts or stages of development which are revealed in attitude and behavior (character traits). Obviously, it is beyond the scope of this text to consider an in-depth theory of cognitive science and psychology. However, it is useful to outline how dedicated mind/body training creates an upward spiral of expanded awareness and increased physical and mental control.

Below are four areas of development, which in the early stages of training, seem to progress sequentially. In time, positive character traits will advance concurrently given their interdependent nature, particularly in the first three areas. The final stage of training is rarely achieved. This is the heart/mind of an enlightened person, who has seen the True Self and the true nature of things. Such a person does not distinguish himself or herself from others.

- Character Traits of Self-Awareness: Self-respect, Self-reflection, Self-esteem
- Character Traits of Intention to Achieve Self-Mastery: Willpower, Patience, Self-control, Confidence
- Character Traits of Seeing Our Interconnectedness: Empathy, Cooperation, Leadership, Advocacy
- Character Traits of Oneness and The Non-Dualistic Mind: A heart/mind devoid of conflict and violence

A. CHARACTER TRAITS OF SELF-AWARENESS

When one begins training, inevitably one's mind is intent on following the instructions of the teacher, as well as understanding the immediate environment—the training hall and the actions of other students. These early days of training require a heightened effort to develop self-awareness. There is a belief among those who know the art of self-defense: The first day of training is the most precious, because it is greeted by a fresh mind or beginner's mind (*sho-shin*). The mind of *sho-shin* is excited to learn. It is unencumbered by preconceptions and complacency. This fresh view of oneself is to be treasured and re-created time and time again, to keep one's training alive and progressing. *Sho-shin* cultivates self-reflection and fosters steady growth (see Chapter 6: *Attitude in Training*).

In addition to the training hall offering a backdrop for seeing one's self, the practice of breathing techniques and concentration (*mokuso*) can be useful on a subtler level by quieting the body and mind enough to reveal certain thought processes and underlying beliefs of oneself. Further, breathing practices have a positive impact physically, as they allow the energy and systems of the body to function harmoniously (see Chapter 7: *The Breath, Energy and Ki-ai*).

There is a saying: "In the practice of self-reflection (*hansei*), it is good to be honest and sincere. The true value of self-reflection is to appreciate the view of one's past actions and to learn from it by diligently applying what knowledge has come from this insight."

Once a person begins to understand himself or herself better, self-respect will grow. Naturally, such a person begins to take responsibility to fulfill his or her potential and will be more eager to take on the task of self-mastery.

A Note About Self-Respect and Self-Esteem: Self-esteem is rooted in our self-concept, and it is developed primarily from feedback from others and from our own self-evaluation. In other words, self-esteem is a product of how we internalize other people's subjective evaluation of our worth, ability or performance, combined with the beliefs we hold about ourselves. Self-respect, however, arises out of a knowledge of *our intrinsic, undeniable value, regardless of one's capabilities*. In time, a mature feeling of self-respect includes a sense of confidence and humility, which develops as we see ourselves as we are.

B. CHARACTER TRAITS OF INTENTION TO ACHIEVE SELF-MASTERY

As mentioned earlier, mastering the wide-ranging, yet exacting, elements in the art of self-defense requires diligent and consistent effort. As proficiency increases, positive character traits inevitably are nurtured and build on each other in an upward spiral. Strength-of-will and self-discipline are the foundations of self-mastery. A great number of positive character traits are directly linked to willpower and self-control, such as confidence, intentionality, concentration, timeliness, temperate speech and, most importantly, patience and perseverance (*nin-tai*). For a deeper discussion of *nin-tai*, see Chapter 6, Section 3.

Specifically regarding a physical exercise regimen and willpower: A recent study by two Australian scientists discovered that volunteers who followed a two-month program of physical exercise—a routine that required willpower "…produced significant improvements in a wide range of regulatory behaviours."[34] It is interesting to note from this study that specifically exerting willpower within a physical exercise regime leads to stronger self-control in nearly all areas of life, such as making healthier choices and increasing concentration.[35]

Specifically, regarding self-control: Self-control may be the single most important character trait as a determinant of health and success. A 30-year study, using data from a cohort of more than 1000 children from New Zealand, demonstrated that measures of childhood self-control taken at ages three

---

[34] Oaten, Megan, and Ken Cheng. "Longitudinal Gains in Self-regulation from Regular Physical Exercise." *British Journal of Health Psychology* 11.4 (2006): 717-33. US National Library of Medicine. Web. 4 Jan. 2017. https://www.ncbi.nlm.nih.gov/pubmed/17032494.

[35] "What You Need to Know about Willpower: The Psychological Science of Self-Control." *American Psychological Association*, 2012. Web. 04 Jan. 2017. http://www.apa.org/helpcenter/willpower.pdf.

through eleven were closely related to adult outcomes in areas as diverse as physical health, income, substance abuse and criminal behavior.[36] This particular study was able to neutralize the mitigating factors of intelligence and socio-economic background. The results of this comprehensive research strongly reinforce the need for one to strive for increased self-control and overall self-mastery.

C. CHARACTER TRAITS OF APPRECIATING OUR INTER-CONNECTEDNESS

"Unless one is strong, one cannot help others."

Self-development progresses when one has a clear commitment to the path of self-mastery, and slowly, he or she will understand the value of helping others. It is undeniable that we are all interconnected and we share an innate desire to grow. When we feel strong, we feel that we can give.

The traditional training floor offers an ideal environment to help others in a healthy, constructive manner, all the while subtlety communicating: "I want to help you, because your life is valuable, and I hope you will be safe and grow alongside everyone here." Often people feel a desire to help others; however, finding a manner in which to do so can be challenging. Tendencies for co-dependency and misguided generosity are commonplace. Self-defense training offers a balanced mechanism that allows one to help others to help themselves (see Chapter 6, Section 1: *Culture and Regimen of the Training Hall*).

D. CHARACTER TRAITS OF ONENESS AND THE NON-DUALISTIC MIND

In time and with much practice, consciousness will expand to perceive that one's life is joined with the universal energy. This state of awareness is selfless and resides in oneness with the universal principle. While it is difficult for the everyday mind to imagine such insight, those who achieve it, emphatically claim that all human beings are meant to live in harmony with one another. No conflict exists in this state of mind, as it experiences life beyond the state of duality. Following is a beautiful description of this enlightened mind from Buddhist priest, Muso Sōseki's *Dialogues in a Dream* (*Muchū Mondō-shū*).

> *Objectless compassion occurs when, following the realization of enlightenment, the compassion that is an inherent virtue of the [True Self] manifests itself and functions naturally to liberate all [living] beings, even when there is no conscious striving to do so. It is like the moon, which equally casts its reflection on water everywhere"* ... thus in spreading the Truth. Here... *"there is no distinction between 'teaching' and 'not teaching' and in liberating people there are no notions of 'benefit' and 'no benefit'.*[37]

---

[36] Moffitt, Terrie E. "A Gradient of Childhood Self-Control Predicts Health, Wealth, and Public Safety." Proceedings of the National Academy of Sciences of the United States of America, National Academy of Sciences, 15 Feb. 2011, www.ncbi.nlm.nih.gov/pmc/articles/PMC3041102/.

[37] Soseki, Muso, and Thomas Yuho Kirchner. *Dialogues in a Dream: The Life and Zen Teachings of Muso Soseki*, Wisdom Publications, 2015, p. 112.

Another description of the non-dualistic mind is found in the following whimsical story from the essential Daoist text, *Zhuangzi*, written by the Chinese philosopher, Zhuang Zhou, who lived around the fourth century BCE.

> *Once, Zhuang Zhou dreamed he was a butterfly, a butterfly flitting and fluttering about, happy with himself and doing as he pleased. He didn't know that he was Zhuang Zhou.*
>
> *Suddenly he woke up and there he was, solid and unmistakable Zhuang Zhou. But he didn't know if he was Zhuang Zhou who had dreamt he was a butterfly, or a butterfly dreaming that he was Zhuang Zhou.*
>
> *Between Zhuang Zhou and the butterfly there must be some distinction!*
> *This is called the Transformation of Things.*[38]

---

[38] Zhuangzi. *Complete Works of Zhuangzi,* translated by Burton Watson, Columbia Univ. Press, 2013, p. 44.

Section 3 – Definition of a "Strong Person"

A strong person is one who has self-control, self-respect and self-confidence. A strong person does not try to control others, but rather demonstrates a quiet confidence.

A strong person is capable of going beyond his/her subjective judgment. In order to choose the right path and make sound decisions, it is important to see clearly what is in front of us. While the ability to be objective is linked to self-control, it also is tied to the capacity to be less self-centered.

In training, it is important to be guided by a code of conduct. In Japanese training schools, this code of conduct is known as the *Dojo Kun*. The *kun* describes two principles: one, the long-term aim of training within the context of the whole of life, and two, it defines the standard of behavior of students in training and in society.

Generally speaking, the *Dojo Kun* marks the path of becoming a person of strong character. The following *kun* is written by Hidy Ochiai for students of his teachings

One who perseveres invites happiness.
In all things, one must be patient and pay effort.
In encounters with others, one must not forget to show respect and to be kind.

The Tale of The Tea Master on the following page illustrates the importance of mental strength, confidence and self-control.

THE TALE OF THE TEA MASTER

A famous tea master of seventeenth-century Japan once insulted a low-positioned samurai by accident. The tea master profusely apologized to the samurai, but the samurai adamantly refused to accept the humble apology. Instead, the samurai demanded that they duel to settle the matter.

The tea master did not know what to do, for he was a man of peace and was not accustomed to fighting. He did not even carry a sword. The samurai, on the other hand, was interested only in fighting and demonstrating his skill in sword fighting. The tea master was finally forced to accept the challenge by the samurai. And so, on the day before the duel, the tea master held a sword for the first time, and someone showed him how to swing it.

Although not familiar with the way of the sword, the tea master was a Zen master as well, and had so cultivated his mind that he was not afraid of death. Before the duel, he meditated in a sitting position for a while, then made tea, which he drank ceremoniously as he always had. His mind was calm and stable.

People gathering for the duel were amazed at the tea master's appearance. The meek-looking man was gone. There stood a man full of pride and confidence. The tea master showed no fear of death. He knew he was right in the eyes of heaven (the gods), and he believed that he could not be defeated by the ill-willed samurai. The tea master's confidence and belief-in-the-self shone in his eyes. The samurai, as soon as he saw the tea master standing proudly and calmly with the sword in his hands, realized that he had challenged the wrong man. He called off the duel and ran away.

This story, of course, illustrates how strength of mind and belief in yourself help prepare you for fighting—and can even overcome a violent situation. Indeed, physical skills are nothing unless they are properly utilized when needed, and only mental strength makes that possible. Mental strength includes self-discipline, self-control, confidence, and respect for yourself and others. A greater ability to concentrate also comes with serious practice. *

---

* Ochiai, Hidy. Hidy Ochiai's Complete Book of Self-Defense. Paperback. 191. Contemporary Books. p. 1.

CHAPTER 5

Perception or "Seeing" in Self-Defense: *Ken* and *Kan*
Levels of Self-defense

The legendary Japanese swordsman, Miyamoto Musashi "describes two kinds of seeing: one with the physical eyes, the other with one's perception and intuition." The first is called *ken*; the second is called *kan*. "*Kan* is the mental vision that is needed to perceive things beyond their physical appearance." *Kan* is the insight into the essence and true meaning of things. Even when one's eyes are open, one can apply *kan* by turning the mind inward to capture the underlying truth. Developing the mind's eye requires effort and training. The stronger a person becomes, the more one's awareness is developed to see the essential truth of the whole situation—thus finding the path for safety and reconciliation. Ultimately, only with *kan*, can one truly know how best to respond to a threat.[39]

Musashi also "warns us that we should not be deceived by physical appearance. It is important for us to cultivate the ability to understand a person or thing in more ways than that which our physical eyes can judge."[40] To put it differently, Musashi is confirming that human beings have the ability to perceive a situation, person or thing with what might be called a *sixth sense*. We call feel or intuit that a situation may be dangerous, even while outwardly it may appear to be fine. This intuitive sense, or *kan*, can capture the essence or intent of another's motives.

A Kind Word Turneth Away Wrath, which follows on the next two pages, is a well-known, true story by aikidoka Terry Dobson (1939-1992). Dobson had been an *uchi-deshi* (live-in student) of aikido founder, Morihei Ueshiba in Japan from about 1959-1964 and continued to train under Master Ueshiba until Ueshiba's death in 1969. The story illustrates what a truly strong person can do with the application of *kan*, patience and kindness.

---

[39] Miyamoto, Musashi. *A Way to Victory: The Annotated Book of Five Rings*. Trans. Hidy Ochiai. New York: Overlook, 2005. 84-85. Print.
[40] Ibid., 5

A KIND WORD TURNETH AWAY WRATH

The train clanks and rattles through the suburbs of Tokyo on a drowsy spring afternoon. Our car was comparatively empty—a few housewives with their kids in tow, some old folks going shopping. I gazed absently at the drab houses and dusty hedgerows.

At one station the doors open, and suddenly the afternoon quiet was shattered by a man bellowing violent, incomprehensible curses. The man staggers into my car. He is wearing laborer's clothing, and he is big, drunk, and dirty. Screaming, he swings at a woman holding a baby. The blow sends her spinning into the laps of an elderly couple. It is a miracle that she's unharmed.

Terrified, the couple jump up and scramble toward the other end of the car. The laborer aims a kick at the retreating back of the old woman but missed as she scuttles to safety. This so enrages the drunk that he grabs the metal pole in the center of the car and tries to wrench it out of its stanchion. I can see that one of his hands is cut and bleeding. The train lurches ahead, the passengers frozen with fear.

I was young then, some twenty years ago, and in pretty good shape. I'd been putting in eight hours of aikido training nearly every day for the past three years. I liked to throw and grapple. I thought I was tough. Trouble was, my martial skill was untested in actual combat. As students of aikido, we were not allowed to fight.

"Aikido," my teacher had said again and again, "is the art of reconciliation. Whoever has the mind to fight has broken his connection with the universe. If you try to dominate people, you are already defeated. We study how to resolve conflict, not how to start it."

I listened to his words. I tried hard I even went so far as to cross the street to avoid the *chimpira*, the pinball punks who lounged around the train stations. My forbearance exalted me. I feel both tough and holy. In my heart, however, I want an absolutely legitimate opportunity whereby I might save the innocent by destroying the guilty.

"This is it!" I say to myself, getting to my feet. People are in danger and if I don't do something fast, they will probably get hurt. Seeing me stand up, the drunk recognizes a chance to focus his rage. "Aha!" He roars. "A foreigner! You need a lesson in Japanese manners!"

I hold on lightly to the commuter strap overhead and give him a slow look of disgust and dismissal. I plan to take this turkey apart, but he has to make the first move. I want him mad, so I pursed my lips and blew him an insolent kiss. "All right!" he hollers. "You're gonna get a lesson." He gathers himself for a rush at me.

A split second before he can move, someone shouted "Hey!" It's earsplitting. I remember the strangely joyous, lilting quality of it—as though you and a friend had been searching diligently for something, and he suddenly stumbled upon it. "Hey!"

I wheel to my left; the drunk spins to his right. We both stare down at a little old Japanese man. He must have been well into his seventies, this tiny gentleman, sitting there immaculate in his kimono. He takes no notice of me, but beams delightedly at the laborer, as though he has a most important, most welcome secret to share.

"C'mere," the old man says in an easy vernacular, beckoning to the drunk. "C'mere and talk with me." He waves his hand lightly.

The big man follows, as if on a string. He plants his feet belligerently in front of the old gentleman, and roars above the clacking wheels, "Why the hell should I talk to you?" The drunk now had his back to me. If his elbow moves so much as a millimeter, I'll drop him in his socks.

The old man continues to beam at the laborer. "What'cha been drinkin'?" he asks, his eyes sparkling with interest. "I been drinkin' sake," the laborer bellows back, "and it's none of your business!" Flecks of spittle spattered the old man.

"Ok, that's wonderful." the old man said, "Absolutely wonderful! You see, I love sake too. Every night, me and my wife—she's seventy-six, you know—we warm up a little bottle of sake and take it out into the garden, and we sit on an old wooden bench. We watch the sun go down, and we look to see how our persimmon tree is doing. My great-grandfather planted that tree, and we worry about whether it will recover from those ice storms we had last winter. Our tree had done better than I expected, though especially when you consider the poor quality of the soil. It is gratifying to watch when we take our sake and go out to enjoy the evening - even when it rains!" He looked up at the laborer, eyes twinkling.

As he struggles to follow the old man's conversation, the drunk's face begins to soften. His fists slowly unclench. "Yeah," he says. "I love persimmons too..." His voice trails off.

"Yes," said the old man, smiling, "and I'm sure you have a wonderful wife."

"No," replies the laborer. "My wife died." Very gently, swaying with the motion of the train, the big man began to sob. "I don't got no wife, I don't got no home, I don't got no job. I am so ashamed of myself." Tears rolled down his cheeks; a spasm of despair ripples through his body. Now it was my turn. Standing there in well-scrubbed youthful innocence, my make-his-world-safe-for-democracy righteousness, I suddenly feel dirtier than he was.

Then the train arrives at my stop. As the doors open, I hear the old man cluck sympathetically. "My, my," he says, "that is a difficult predicament, indeed. Sit down here and tell me about it."

I turn my head for one last look. The laborer sprawled on the seat, his head in the old man's lap. The old man was softly stroking the filthy, matted hair. As the train pulls away, I sit down on a bench. What I'd wanted to do with muscle had been accomplished with kind words. I had just seen aikido tried in combat, and the essence of it was love. I would have to practice the art with an entirely different spirit. It would be a long time before I could speak about the resolution of conflict.

This story was first published in the Lomi School Bulletin, Summer 1980, pp. 23-24 © Terry Dobson under the title, *A Kind Word Turneth Away Wrath*.* The version printed here is an excerpt from a book written Dobson's partner, Riki Moss, which is based on the writings and recordings of Terry Dobson.**

* Strozzi-Heckler, Richard, et al. *Aikido and the New Warrior*. North Atlantic Books, 1985. Acknowledgments page.
** Riki Moss and Terry Dobson (2009). An *Obese White Gentleman in No Apparent Distress*. Blue Snake Books. pp. 43-47.

Section 1 – Level One: Mental Self-Defense (The Advanced Guard)

Mental self-defense requires on-going discipline to remain aware and use common sense to steer away from potential danger, even if none is apparent. It is important to know our environment, which includes the spaces we traverse in our everyday life, as well as new environments, such as identifying potential danger areas. For example, jogging along a busy road in your neighborhood during daylight hours might seem safe enough, but it is not safe if the pathway is lined with a dense hedgerow on one side. If one is out for an evening stroll to a nearby grocery shop, choosing a path along a well-lit street is always a better choice than a dark shortcut. One lesson of effective self-defense training is to recognize that we are never separate from our physical environment.

> *In applying one's knowledge of self-defense to daily life, it is useful to remember that the best defense is to need no defense at all. Prevention of a crisis is a far greater measure of wisdom than treatment.*

While a person can learn mental self-defense at any age, the most effective way to learn the necessary skill is to practice it systematically from a young age. Development of mental self-defense skills happens gradually, and it is closely linked to one's self-worth. As an individual grows to adulthood, mental self-defense must continue to be polished to adapt to new worldly environments.

Possibly one of the most important elements of self-defense is a commitment to not misuse drugs, alcohol, or other mind-altering substances. Countless lives have been needlessly lost and ruined by drug and alcohol abuse. When under the influence of drugs, one is not in control of oneself, physically or mentally, and the likelihood of making poor decisions increases. Keeping an attitude of anti-drugs, anti-violence and respect will always lead to greater potential for success in life.

In the totality of one's life span, mental self-defense is certainly more important than the ability to defend oneself physically. Through strengthening the mind-body connection and physical skill in self-defense training, one will acquire a heightened ability for mental self-defense in everyday life. Increased self-respect and respect for others will spontaneously dictate action toward safer choices and non-violent resolutions to conflict.

The wisdom of philosopher Cheng Yi (1033-1107 CE) echoes a subtle principle in mental self-defense.

> *The point is that when strength is not balanced correctly it behaves impulsively; it does not stay peacefully in place.*
>
> *Because it is not balanced correctly it is not steady; and it is precisely this insecurity that makes it contentious. If you do not press any contention that you should not press, and go back to find out the real truth, you will change insecurity into security, which is fortunate.* [41]

---

[41] Tzu, Sun, and Thomas Cleary. *The Art of War: Complete Texts and Commentaries*, Shambhala Publications, 2005, p. 200.

Simple everyday choices can have a profound impact on our safety. Some general rules for mental self-defense are:

1. *Pay attention to the path of your life and make choices to further well-being.* It can't be overstated that mental self-defense begins with paying attention to what one is doing at the moment and making good decisions. Many injuries happen because of carelessness, lack of attention and indifference.

    Watch where you're going. Of the top ten causes of death in the United States in 2020, the single largest *non-disease related* cause of death was accidents. Unintentional injuries placed fourth in front of stroke, Alzheimer's disease and diabetes. Approximately 200,955 people died in 2020 from unintentional injuries, which include opioid overdoses (unintentional poisoning), motor vehicle crashes, and unintentional falls.[42]

    According to the mortality data from the National Center for Health Statistics (NCHS) at the Centers for Disease Control and Prevention (CDC), in 2020, approximately 40,698 people died because of a fall, representing 12.8 percent of all injury-related deaths.[43] Walking in a busy urban setting is potentially dangerous, even without considering a potential attack from another. Carelessly crossing streets, not paying attention our surroundings or where we are stepping, can result not only in our falling, but also our contributing to the fall of another.

2. *Do not use drugs unless medically necessary.* Further mortality data from the NCHS at the CDC, unintentional poisoning was the leading cause of accidental deaths in 2020, when 87,404 people died from accidental poisoning, primarily from the misuse of legal and illegal drugs, as well as from medically prescribed drugs. This statistic representing 26.5 percent of all injury-related deaths.[44]

3. Do not use misuse alcohol and be cautious of those who have had too much to drink. "Every day, about 32 people in the United States die in drunk-driving crashes — that's one person every 45 minutes. In 2020, 11,654 people died in alcohol-impaired driving traffic deaths — a 14% increase from 2019. These deaths were all preventable."[45] Further, many of the worst incidents of domestic violence are caused by the abuse of alcohol.

4. *Define and control your boundaries, particularly with strangers.* There are relatively few circumstances which require a stranger to approach another person, purposefully. Individuals with malice often have a method for getting inside another's boundaries to target potential victims. Always be ready to question the intention of an approaching stranger.

---

[42] Murphy SL, Kochanek KD, Xu JQ, Arias E. Mortality in the United States, 2020. NCHS Data Brief, no 427. Hyattsville, MD: National Center for Health Statistics. 2021, p. 4. https://www.cdc.gov/nchs/data/databriefs/db427.pdf.
[43] Centers for Disease Control and Prevention, National Center for Health Statistics. National Vital Statistics System, Mortality 1999-2020 on CDC WONDER Online Database, released in 2021. Data are from the Multiple Cause of Death Files, 1999-2020, as compiled from data provided by the 57 vital statistics jurisdictions through the Vital Statistics Cooperative Program. Accessed at http://wonder.cdc.gov/ucd-icd10.html
[44] Ibid.
[45] "Drunk Driving." NHTSA, US Department of Transportation, https://www.nhtsa.gov/risky-driving/drunk-driving.

Instinctively, most of us keep a natural distance from strangers, such as in a waiting room or at a bus stop. But, in those situations where one must be close to others, it is important to be vigilant and to engage all one's senses.

5. *Do not act like a victim.* Predators look for specific traits in their would-be victims, such as lack of confidence displayed in body language and lack of alertness to the surroundings. Weakness is conveyed in our posture, motions and eyes. It's important to project inner strength, to stand straight with confidence and to walk purposefully with one's head up.

    It's also best to keep one's hands free and out of pockets. Today's constant use of hand-held devices and earphones in public spaces is a predator's dream.

    Remember that violent individuals are not looking for a "fair fight" but rather seeking a situation they believe that they can firmly control. By simply changing certain aspects of how we behave in public, we are already warding off potential attacks.

6. *Respect for parents, teachers and those who genuinely care for us.* When children pay attention to guidance from caring parents, relatives and teachers, the chance for these children to develop poor attitudes and behaviors is reduced. Of course, there are some regrettable cases that caution us not to make too generalized a statement. It is possible for bad adults to exist within families. Children must be encouraged to believe in themselves, to trust their own feelings and to stand up for what they believe is right. In this way children can be guided correctly. Children who are afraid to express themselves may be more vulnerable.

7. *The importance throughout one's life of choosing good friends.* This is an often-forgotten rule in the lives of children AND adults. True friends want to help others achieve their potential. Good people can be swayed to make bad choices when under the influence of dishonest, manipulative peers. Even the most grounded and steady young person can be targeted and victimized by sophisticated manipulations of dangerous predatory people or cults.

Section 2 – Level Two: Establishing Distance from Perceived Danger

When one perceives that danger may be present, one's awareness will instantly be heightened. The *first and most important concern* must be to create distance—a "safety zone" between oneself and the perceived threat. If establishing a safe distance is not immediately possible, then using all one's resources (engaging the help of others, distraction, a loud voice, grabbing a protective device, and so on) to prevent the danger from escalating is critical.

It is a physiological fact that someone must be in close proximity to another person to do physical harm. There are exceptions to this rule; for example, a situation that involves a weapon, such as a handgun. However, even in this case, distance will improve the odds of a safe resolution, particularly if the attacker is not within a close range at the start of the encounter.

Therefore, a "safety zone" is a specific type of boundary that best neutralizes an identified danger in any given circumstance. For example, establishing a safe distance might be to drive away in a car or to run away to a nearby structure. In cases of home intruders, families may be wise to establish a safe, concealed space in the house that has an adequate phone connection to dial 911 where children and adults can hide.

Section 3 – Level Three: Surviving Physical Assault

This final level of self-defense is what everyone should work to avoid at all costs. When mental self-defense and establishing a safety zone have failed, one will be forced to physically defend oneself and potentially win a life-or-death battle. At this point, one must fight with the *total-self*, without fear or hesitation, with one thing in mind: *to protect oneself*.

The split-second decisions that one makes in the first moments of such an encounter can be the difference between life and death. Two things should be a top priority to better one's odds for survival. One, do everything possible to avoid being abducted. Do not allow yourself to be taken to a secondary location, such as being forced into a car, an alley or a building. Two, if you are in a hand-to-hand fight, do not let yourself be taken to the ground; remain upright, if possible. In other words, avoid a ground-fighting interaction with an attacker.

Of course, it goes without saying that one should use all the self-defense techniques that one has learned. Do whatever it takes to free oneself to get to safety. Overcoming the aggression of an attacker requires concentrated willpower and strategic decision making. One's mindset must be to see oneself as a victor, and not as a victim!

CHAPTER 6

Attitude in Training
Key Elements for Developing Proper Attitude in Training

Learning physical self-defense techniques is a systematic, predictable process. However, as we have seen, these physical techniques are a relatively small part of total self-defense theory. The real challenge in the study of self-defense is to find a training method which presents effective physical techniques while concurrently cultivating sound judgment and positive character traits.

In traditional martial arts, something known as *shin-gi-tai* (mind/character, technique and body) is highly valued. Not developing one's mind and character alongside physical techniques can actually be counterproductive and dangerous, as these techniques are to be used solely for non-violent purposes. The harmonization of one's mind, character, skill and physical techniques allow one to demonstrate civility and compassion, and to use the art of self-defense to restore safety and peace.

Section 1 – Culture and Regimen of the Training Hall

Refining physical techniques in a prescribed, purposeful manner can transform the individual's mind and character. In this method, *physiology creates psychology*. The transformation happens on several levels: the training hall environment, the practice of breathing, overall physical conditioning, the practice of stance and posture, maintaining correct intention in practice, proper attitude in the training hall and in daily life.

A. First, the total training environment, i.e. the "culture on the training floor," is far more critical to a successful training method than one might imagine. A training floor must be safe, gender neutral, courteous and singular in focus. When an individual enters the training floor, he or she will instantly receive a serious message from the attitudes of the fellow trainees. If those on the floor are practicing with an attitude of respect and display a commitment to the overall betterment of everyone on the floor, including themselves, the "collective training mind" will have the correct focus, i.e. the growth in each individual and the development of proficiency in technique. It is the instructor's and students' duty to ensure that the correct focus and attitude is always maintained on the floor. Traditional self-defense training *is based on respect for each individual's capability.*

Further, maintaining a clean and safe environment is essential to a healthy training hall and is *the responsibility of everyone in the school*. This not only applies to careful execution of techniques and mindfulness of others' abilities, it is demonstrated by basic courtesy, such as keeping personal cleanliness (finger nails and toenails short and uniform washed). The floor and training equipment should be regularly cleaned.

B. Second, an essential element of a sound practice method is standing or sitting for a few minutes with a straight spine together with quiet, controlled breathing to allow the energy within the body to flow correctly. The practice of establishing a quiet body and quiet mind (*mokuso*) before training has been fundamental to traditional self-defense and martial arts disciplines for centuries (see Chapter 7: *The Breath, Energy and Ki-ai*).

C. Third, regular aerobic exercise is also important. It's a well-known fact that exercise positively impacts all the biological systems of the human body, such as brain function and cognition, respiration, circulation, hormonal balance and musculoskeletal strength—all of which lead to the overall well-being of the individual. Exercise also increases physical stamina and heightens awareness of one's true abilities.

D. Fourth, the significance of "intention in practice" cannot be understated. The true value from training is found in the sincerity and concentration of one's effort. Half-hearted training will not result in meaningful self-development. Therefore, it is important to set aside worldly concerns temporarily, in order to maintain a singular focus of doing one's best on the training floor. This will benefit you and your training partners.

E. Fifth, many of the basic techniques in this book are aimed at increasing self-awareness by working with stance and outwardly relating these physical postures with psychological attributes, such as respect, confidence and concentration. Diligently practicing techniques with strong postures, stances and correct breathing methods will strengthen the tie between one's physical and mental state, gradually increasing one's self-control.

The practice of mind-body training doesn't end when one leaves the training hall. It continues. Proficiency in any art requires constant, diligent effort, and the art of self-defense is no exception (see Chapter 10: *Strengthening the Mind-body Connection*).

SELF-DEFENSE CREED

- The strength of a person is measured not by how much one can control others, but rather by how much one can control one's self.

- Violence has no place in a human society. The denial of violence must include an ability to defend oneself against violent acts. The highest aim in any self-defense situation is to stop the aggression, defuse conflict, while injuring no one.

- One should *never* provoke a violent confrontation.

- Mental self-defense is more important than the ability to defend oneself physically.

- *Get away. Run away. Right Away.* The first technique of self-defense is to escape. Quickly leaving the scene of a potentially dangerous situation, regardless of one's capability to defend oneself, is fundamental to self-defense. Ego and curiosity should not interfere with this principle.

- Use physical techniques only as the last resort. Diligent practice of sound physical self-defense techniques may give one a chance to prevail when applied with a full fighting spirit in most violent confrontations.

- Practice *onko chishin*: "Respect the knowledge of what has been learned in the past, so as to learn and integrate new knowledge wisely." Originally, found in the Analects of Confucius, the Japanese adage of *onko chishin* (Chinese: *wēn gù zhī xīn*) conveys a right path for living.

  Do not under-estimate the value of learning from the experience of those who have lived ahead of us. Obviously, this includes those who have lived with wisdom and strong character, including the great philosophers and sages, and our immediate predecessors.

  Equally important, however, is to learn from the mistakes of those who have not lived wisely and have made poor choices. A clear example of this is recognizing the countless lives that have been lost or destroyed by the misuse of drugs and alcohol. Intentionally putting one's self in an impaired mental state can often lead to making an irreversible mistake.

Section 2 – *Sho-shin*

In Japan, the word *sho-shin*, is literally translated as "beginner's mind." This author feels this translation does not fully convey the spirit of this important concept; therefore, he uses the words "fresh mind" to clarify the meaning of *sho-shin*. *Sho-shin* is a guiding concept for everyone who strives for progress in his or her art. In self-defense training, one is encouraged to confront psychological weaknesses such as being irresolute, angry, and complacent. *Sho-shin* allows one to engage wholeheartedly in training with sincerity, courtesy, diligence and continued self-awareness.

When the mind is too occupied with ideas and preconceptions, it often ceases to absorb new and important information. Bringing *sho-shin* to a task or circumstance allows one's mind to be open and willing to learn, with a sense of humility and excitement. *Sho-shin* is applicable to every facet of life.

> *Sho-shin awakens an energy which is only found in the excitement and focus of seeing something for the first time.*

Over time, as one studies a subject or art form, the mind becomes richer with knowledge and understanding; but at the same time, it can become clouded with arrogance, assumptions and old impressions. Such a mind no longer sees things clearly and directly, and it often ceases to absorb new and important things.

An ancient saying is that a cup full of tea cannot hold any more. Therefore, one's mind (cup) must be empty and ready to accept new knowledge for the constant improvement and progress in self-development. When one truly engages in learning with a fresh mind, a sense of humility will automatically follow.

Section 3 – *Nin-tai*: Determination to Practice with Patience and Perseverance

An inherent principle in learning effective self-defense techniques is constant and *correct* practice. The practice of the basics in any art requires patience and perseverance, and the art of self-defense is no exception.

Hundreds of repetitions of a single technique are required. The repetitive training needed to master techniques can become boring for an undisciplined mind. Therefore, training in the art of self-defense presents an opportunity for one to develop strength of character, through *nin-tai* (self-discipline, patience and perseverance).

In a more philosophical but also very real manner, patience, in and of itself, when applied to a potentially volatile encounter can be a self-defense technique. The importance of inner strength developed in training cannot be overestimated. For example, if in an everyday social encounter, one is insulted for no apparent reason, one can apply *nin-tai to* simply dismiss the potentially explosive situation.

Section 4 – *Kaizen*: Constant Improvement and Self-Competition

Kaizen means "constant improvement." Historically, this word primarily has been applied in Japan to business organizations and the manufacturing processes, as a philosophy to maintain quality-control and effective management systems. However, this author believes that kaizen is an important tool for individual self-development.

Central to the practice of *kaizen* is the word "constant." To constantly improve, one must maintain self-awareness, apply *sho-shin* (fresh mind) in each moment, and work with patience and diligence. *Kaizen* is primarily an inner striving. If one really wants to get value out of self-defense training, one should direct the competitive attitude inward; in other words, toward the self.

Self-competition is the toughest kind of competition, as it requires one to look at the self from an objective viewpoint, and it never ends. Whether it entails improving areas of strength or facing and transforming areas of weaknesses, there can be no end to self-improvement.

Section 5 – Intention: "Practice as if it's real."

An important mental tool in achieving the most from the practice of each technique is to imagine that it is a real self-defense situation. Each escape, block, parry and counterattack should be performed with the full intention, applying the required focus and power to succeed.

Note: It goes without saying that even though one is practicing as if it's real, safety must be of paramount importance. Therefore, practicing with full intention requires self-discipline and a careful consideration of one's surroundings.

Section 6 – Safety

The importance of safety must be cultivated in the minds of those on the training floor. It is the responsibility of the participants to maintain a safe environment, and through the cultivation of mutual respect, productive and safe self-defense training can be achieved.

A primary means to maintain safety in training is to respect individual capability—physical, mental and emotional. Each person enters the floor with a unique set of strengths and weaknesses. The purpose of training is to develop awareness and respect among trainees, so that everyone can progress in the art of self-defense.

CHAPTER 7

The Breath, Energy and *Ki-ai*

Section 1 – Importance of Breath

For millennia, traditional cultures have understood the importance of the breath. Some describe "life" entering and leaving the body "on the breath," as if the life-force itself is linked inseparably to breathing. While the human body can live for weeks without food and days without water, it can only survive a few minutes without the breath. Further, these ancient cultures valued the transformative power of the breath to develop overall physical and mental well-being. In-depth discussions of breathing practice and the benefits of these techniques can be found in many ancient texts, such as the *Upanishads*, the *Vedas*, Lao Tzu's *Tao Te Ching*, Aristotle's *On Breath*, and Patanjali's *Yoga Sutras*.[46]

To some extent, this profound appreciation of correct breathing techniques has survived to modern times in a handful of art forms and disciplines. Unfortunately, in our world today, the cultivation of good breathing habits is not taught as a necessity for everyday living. The breath is one of two fundamental vehicles which supply "nutrition" to the body—the other being food/water. In a sense, the breath is the principal vehicle of sustenance in that, before the cells access nutrients in food, they must have oxygen.

Correct breathing methods are essential to developing mental, emotional and physical control, and eventually to establishing harmony of mind and body. To become truly proficient in the art of self-defense, it is important to incorporate breathing exercises in one's training regimen. For example, the difference between a person who panics and one who remains calm in a crucial situation may have its roots in the individual's breathing method. This fact is demonstrated by the appearance of uneven and irregular breathing patterns when one experiences moments of anger, frustration or extreme fear.

When practicing systematic breathing exercises, it is important to remember that all exercises should be practiced according to one's individual pace. Following the methods patiently and carefully as described will allow the muscles involved in breathing to gradually become strong, which will lead to strengthening the entire body and increasing mental clarity and control.

---

[46] Nair, Sreenath. *Restoration of Breath: Consciousness and Performance*. Amsterdam: Rodopi, 2007. Print.

Section 2 – Practice of *Mokuso* ("Quiet Body, Quiet Mind"): Preparing the Mind for Training

Establishing a "Quiet Body, Quiet Mind" is an important preparation for training. Correct breathing maintains proper balance of the mind and body. It is also vital to making correct focus in techniques. For example, when performing kata (form), a general rule is to inhale during preparation of techniques and to exhale at the moment of the execution of techniques. Historically, *mokuso* was most often performed in the kneeling or seated position to prepare the mind for training. However, because these postures are not comfortable or possible for everyone, the Standing Breathing Technique, discussed in the next section of this chapter, is useful and it affords similar benefits. *Mokuso* should be practiced for one to three minutes. It can be practiced longer, if one is comfortable.

Mokuso [Figures 1-2]

Figs. 1-2 In the beginning, sitting in a simple kneeling posture—this posture is known as *seiza*—with the back straight, and hands gently resting on the thighs with the eyes slightly and softly open.

Mokuso: **Alternate Hand Position [Figures 3]**

Fig. 3   To further the practice of *mokuso*, a more traditional hand position can be taken with the right hand resting on the thighs, gently holding the left hand in its palm. The tips of the thumbs touch lightly to form an oval or can be allowed to fold inward upon each other as shown. The eyes can be slightly open or gently closed. The mouth is gently closed with the tongue lightly placed on the back of the top front teeth.

Section 3 – Standing Breathing Technique (Preparation and Practice)

PREPARATION: In preparation for the standing breathing technique, it is useful to do one or both of the following simple mind/body/breath coordination exercises. In these movements, one takes large, deep inhalations and complete full exhalations—bringing the air fully to the bottom of the lungs upon inhalation and expelling the air completely on exhalation. This oxygenates the cells of the body, while joining the mind, body and breath. *In these preparatory exercises, the inhalation is through the nostrils and the exhalation is through the mouth.*

Preparation #1 for Standing Breathing Technique [Figures 1-4]

Figs. 1-2 Stand in natural stance. Inhale while bringing the arms to the sides with palms facing out and expanding the chest.

Figs. 3-4 Exhale while bringing the arms in front, turning the palms inward, and allowing the head to come down in a relaxed, gentle motion.

Preparation #2 for Standing Breathing Technique [Figures 1-4]

Figs. 1-2 Stand in natural stance. Inhale while bringing the arms to the sides with palms facing out and expanding the chest.

Figs. 3-4 Exhale while going into a full squat, with the arms inside the knees and the head down.

PRACTICE: The practice of the Standing Breathing Technique is used to establish "Quiet Body, Quiet Mind" in preparation for self-defense training. It increases self-awareness and develops a calmer state of mind. This exercise can be used in place of *mokuso*, particularly for beginning students or for those who cannot sit comfortably. It's also useful in training environments where the traditional seated posture is not practical.

Standing Breathing Technique [Figures 1-2]

Figs.1-2   Stand in natural stance with the shoulders and face muscles relaxed, the hands hanging by the sides, and the eyes half-closed with the gaze directed about six feet ahead on the   floor, allowing the eyes to relax in a natural way. Breathe slowly and quietly through the nose. The mind should maintain awareness of the breath at the nostrils.

In this meditative breathing exercise, both the inhalation and the exhalation are through the nostrils.

NOTE: This technique can also be performed seated in a chair with the back straight, and the hands placed flat on the thighs. An alternate hand position for the kneeling posture is to fold the hands within themselves and touch the abdomen with the small fingers.

Section 4 – *Tanden*

In traditional self-defense and martial arts training, the *tanden* is identified as the source of strength and vital energy. The *tanden*, which literally translates as "medicine field," is described as the center of power of the individual. Within the *tanden*, the mind, body and breath can be joined to create a center of strength for the individual to act.

While historical literature identifies several *tanden within* the human body, the primary *tanden* referenced in self-defense training is the lower *tanden* (*ge-tanden*). The lower *tanden* establishes the center of gravity and is the foundation of stance, breath and awareness.

Section 5 – *Ki-ai*: Definition, Practice and Use

In Japan, *ai* means to meet or to join. When *ki* is used in the context of self-defense training, it identifies the power or focused energy that emanates from each individual. *Ki-ai*, which is pronounced *Kee-I*, expresses the power of harmonized mental and physical focus at moment of the execution of technique. *Ki-ai* can be expressed as the forceful exhalation of air (using the *tan-den* or lower abdomen) at this moment of execution. *Ki-ai* most often manifests as the strong, confident shout.

When practicing *ki-ai,* it is particularly important to breathe correctly. The most powerful *ki-ai* is short and explosive and originates in the *tanden*. This is delivered simultaneously with a strong exhalation of air through the mouth. The short *ki-ai* must be executed at the exact moment of the punch, kick or strike, just as fire is ignited when two stones are struck against each other. Actually, this technique is used by many athletes to maximize performance effectiveness, although it is not called *ki-ai* in these instances.

Proper executed *ki-ai* will augment the power and focus of techniques, while simultaneously bringing the abdominal area into a hardened and more protected state. Generally, *ki-ai* is used when delivering a counterattack, especially when one intends it to be the finishing technique, as if to draw on all the available resources within oneself in order to succeed. Through *ki-ai* the muscles and nerves of the body will be concentrated at the moment of sharp mental focus.

Philosophically, *ki-ai* is an expression of the "totality of the self." The practice of *ki-ai* enhances self-confidence and brings out additional energy from within.

CHAPTER 8

Basic Format for Self-Defense Training Sessions

While the two basic formats for self-defense training sessions outlined in this chapter provide a sound method for teaching self-defense, the formats are not set in stone. It will be up to the instructor to decide which elements to emphasize and which elements to occasionally leave out. For example, it may be prudent to focus a single class entirely on a certain self-defense technique while reducing kata practice to a few repetitions. Conversely, it may be useful to spend a good portion of class on blocking only, leaving out any particular self-defense technique. This is what is referred to as the "art of teaching" - matching the class presentation to the needs of the students. An instructor's capacity in this art is directly determined by their ability as a teacher and their knowledge of the curriculum.

Section 1 – Class Format for Teaching Self-Defense to Children in a School Setting

Each class session should have time allotted for basic elements. The basic elements are warm-ups, mini-class discussions, introduction and practice of kata and self-defense techniques, and optional review of techniques.

The following example is the format for a basic training session:

1. Line-up and bow
2. Warm up
3. "Quiet Body, Quiet Mind" Practice
4. Discussion (optional and may be placed later in class time)
5. Kata Practice
6. Review of stances and defensive techniques (optional)
7. Introduction and practice of self-defense technique(s)
8. Cool down
9. Line-up and bow

1. The demonstration of "respect for one's self" and of "mutual respect" is essential to start off every training session. Begin <u>all</u> self-defense training sessions with the students lined-up next to each other in attention stance, facing the instructor (see Chapter 9, Section 2). The instructor faces the group in their formal line-up and then calls out *"rei,"* instructing them to bow and show respect for each other to set the tone for the training session.

2.   After the bow, the teacher has the option to go straight to warm-ups or to present discussion topics to the group, which should take anywhere from a couple of minutes to 15 minutes, depending on the topic(s). For example, the first couple of lessons may include more lengthy discussion sections, as it is important to familiarize the class with key elements of self-defense training (see below), whereas lessons towards the middle and/or end of the curriculum may be much shorter, such as reminders of safety and the importance of patience. In addition, some lessons may not have a designated discussion time at all.

Discussion is an important part of teaching the key elements of self-defense training and should include:

     i. Philosophy of self-defense
     ii. Levels of self-defense
     iii. *Sho-shin* (fresh-mind or beginner's mind)
     iv. Self-development
     v. Self-awareness
     vi. Mind-body connection
     vii. Stances and posture —The foundation of self-defense training
     viii. The importance of breathing — "Quiet Body, Quiet Mind"
     ix. Physical elements of self-defense
     x. Ethical principle of self-defense (see Chapter 1)

3.   When the instructor leads the group in the warm-up session, it should last approximately 5-10 minutes to prepare the body for exercises that will be used later and to prevent injuries by lubricating joints and increasing blood flow to the muscles.

4.   Once the warm-up has been completed, the class should move to the practice of kata or form (see Chapter 16: *Kata*) which should take 10-15 minutes. However, for students, who are just beginning, it will be necessary to use this time slot to introduce or to review the basic stances and the fundamentals of punching and blocking, because these are the building blocks of proper kata. After the class has sufficiently learned these three basic elements, then kata practice can be part of each class. Keep in mind that instead of kata practice, basic stances, punching and blocking should be reviewed vigorously in classes for longer periods of time. This will reinforce attention to detail and to counteract sloppiness and complacency.

5.   Review is always an important part of any training regimen. It cultivates confidence in students, and it offers an opportunity, not only to polish techniques, but to also practice *shoshin* (fresh mind) and *nin-tai* (patience and perseverance).

6.   Now the class is ready to move to self-defense technique(s) for 15-25 minutes. Some lessons may focus on only one self-defense technique and some may examine multiple techniques. Lessons for beginning students should focus more on basic self-defense techniques with fewer moves and only one attacker. As the students advance in their training and knowledge, the introduction of more

complex techniques with one or more attackers can be introduced. Remember to ALWAYS introduce *ukemi*, falling technique (see Chapter 18: *Ukemi*) before any self-defense technique that includes a sweep or throw. Safety is of utmost importance in all self-defense training sessions.

Review self-defense techniques taught in earlier lessons ensures that students are retaining what they have learned. Constant repetition is an essential part of self-defense training. It is the quality of what a student knows, not the quantity that matters in self-defense training. With this in mind, some lessons may consist entirely of techniques taught earlier, and some lessons may contain a technique from an earlier lesson, as well as a new technique. In the latter case, review the "older" technique first, before introducing the new technique.

7. Before ending class, there should be a brief cool down session. The cool down should be no more than 5 minutes and can include breathing exercises, gentle stretches, soft and slow repetition of a kata, and/or the standing breathing technique. The focus of cool down is to provide a pathway the for mind and body to resume normal function—muscle tension, nervous system, heart rate, breath rate and blood pressure.

8. End each training session with a "demonstration of respect" by lining up and bowing as in the beginning of class. This reminds the students of the proper attitude in training and offers a brief practice of the Mind-Body Connection Exercise (see Chapter 10).

Section 2 – Class Format for Teaching Self-Defense to Adults

In a self-defense geared for college students, the basic elements remain the same – warm-ups, mini-class discussions, introduction and practice of kata and self-defense techniques, and optional review of techniques; however, the order and timing of when techniques are presented is more flexible. For example, the warm-ups and "quiet body, quiet mind" practice will commonly precede the initial line-up and bow. The discussion time is often at the conclusion of class it may include a mini lecture of video on specific topics. As noted previously, the line-up and bow to show respect is not as essential at the beginning of class.

The following example is the format for a basic training session:

1. Warm up
2. "Quiet Body, Quiet Mind" Practice
3. Line-up and bow
4. Kata Practice
5. Discussion (optional and may be placed after final line-up and bow)
6. Review of stances and defensive techniques (optional)
7. Introduction and practice of self-defense technique(s)
8. Cool down
9. Line-up and bow

CHAPTER 9

Stances (*Tachikata*)

To deliver a strong and effective technique one must develop a strong and stable stance. Through trial and error, martial arts masters in earlier times developed different stances for different techniques. These stances are the foundations of self-defense techniques.

> *The manner in which the feet hold the ground reflects strength in character, in attitude and in technique.*

Like a magnificent building, which will collapse if its foundation is weak, an impressive martial arts technique is useless if it's executed from a weak and unstable stance. Unlike the foundation of a static structure, stances are constantly shifting to support a kinetic series of motions in self-defense training. Moving from one stance to the next requires balance and control of the whole body during and after the execution of techniques, whether defensive or offensive.

Establishing correct stance is not only a critical part of learning physical self-defense techniques; it is also intrinsic to the development of a strong mental state. The mind and body are interconnected. A stable stance is a manifestation of a strong, confident mind.

Section 1 – Elements of a Strong and Proper Stance

An important aspect for achieving proper stance is muscle tension. There are three primary categories of stances with regard to muscle tension—the natural stances, the outward tension stances and the inward tension stances.

In the natural stances, the muscles of the legs and hips are essentially relaxed, holding only enough tension to keep the body upright and to align the torso, neck and head. These stances are neutral and are used as preparatory postures for moving into another stance, which will support a defensive or offensive technique. Natural stances, while appearing simple, are arguably the most profound of all stances. They represent both the possibility and the readiness to respond to any attack or event that occurs in life.

The inward and outward tension stances keep the legs under tension to maintain balance and strength for executing techniques. Stances such as cat stance and hour glass stance have an inward tension, where the legs feel as if the knees are pressing inward toward each other. Stances like front stance, back stance, and sumo (or stamping) stance have an outward tension, where the knees feel as if they are actively being pushed away from each other.

However, each stance has a counterbalancing tension as well. For example, in front stance, while the front knee is being pushed out, the legs are also being pressed together. In cat stance, it is true that the legs are tensed towards one another, but the back knee must also not cave in, and so it requires a certain amount of power to be pressed outward.

> *Natural stance (hachiji-dachi), while appearing simple, is the most profound of all stances. It is a physically and mentally neutral posture, which represents the readiness to respond effectively to any challenging situation in life.*

Another key aspect of performing any stance well is engaging the feet and toes fully in the stance. In the natural stances, the toes press the ground slightly, as if ready to move to another stance.

In the tension stances, the toes actively "bite" the ground in order to increase balance and stability. There are some martial art masters who do exercises specifically to strengthen their toes, such as rolling newspapers and magazines only using their feet.

As a general rule, when forming a good stance, one's shoulders are relaxed, one's knees are not locked, and one's upper body is comfortably perpendicular to the ground. In training, it is important to practice the various stances described in this book in a series of combined moves. Such sequences might include moving from natural stance to front stance, from straddle stance to back stance and so on; each time assuming the stance by shifting the center of gravity, gripping the ground with the toes and focusing power at the *tanden* (see Chapter 7, Section 4: *Tanden*).

Section 2 – Attention Stances (*Musubi-dachi* and *Heisoku-dachi*)

Attention Stance (*Musubi-dachi*) [Figures 1-3]

Figs. 1-3 Place the heels together. Open the feet 45 degrees in each direction.

Attention Stance (*Heisoku-dachi*) [Figures 4-6]

Figs. 4-6 Place the feet together in parallel. Keep the knees straight but relaxed. Pull the chin in slightly and keep the mouth closed with quiet, stable breathing through the nose. Maintain an awareness of strength in the lower abdomen.

NOTE: In attention stance, the back should be straight with shoulders relaxed and eyes focused on one point. This stance is conducive to a feeling of self-respect. Additionally, bowing from attention stance is a symbolic gesture which shows respect for others.

Section 3 – Attention Stance and Bow (*Rei*)

In self-defense training, the act of bowing, or *rei*, is an important gesture which conveys respect, gratitude and humility for knowledge, which has come from traditional teachers before us. When practicing, it is necessary to show proper respect to your practice partner. Here, the bow is an expression of mutual respect. Although in a real situation one is defending against an attacker, in practice it is a partner who helps you to make progress in the art of self-defense. The mutual bow distinguishes your action from violence and demonstrates respect.

Attention Stance with Bow [Figures 1-3]

Figs. 1-3   Place the heels together. Open the feet 45 degrees in each direction. Bend slowly forward from the hips, keeping the neck in line with the spine. The gaze naturally falls about 4 to 5 feet to the front. Lift the head and raise the upper body back to its original position.

Attention Stance with Mutual Bow [Figures 4-5]

Figs. 4-5   Face each other in attention stance. Bend slowly forward from the hips and direct the eyes forward. Return the upper body to its original position.

Section 4 – Natural Stance (*Shizen-tai* or *Hachiji-dachi*)

Natural stance appears to be the easiest of all stances and its importance is often overlooked. As you study self-defense that is based on traditional martial arts wisdom, you will learn the vital aspects of this stance.

Natural stance is the preparatory form as well as the finishing one. It is also referred to as "mercury's standing method." Mercury is easily and quickly diffused, but when the droplets gather together again, they quickly reconstitute themselves as a whole. Similarly, your initial natural stance should be ready to move in any direction at any time. Movement to and from natural stance is in harmony with your will and in accordance with the needs of the situation you confront.

Importantly, the shoulders must be relaxed, and you must feel the power in the lower abdomen or *tanden* (the area approximately 2 ½ below the navel). As you assume natural stance, you should keep your head upright and direct your eyes forward. The chin should be pulled in slightly in a natural way. Breathing should be quiet and flow evenly as you inhale and exhale through your nose. Power should be felt in the legs, but without applied tension.

Natural Stance (*Shizen-tai* or *Hachiji-dachi*) [Figures 1-3]

Figs. 1-3 Open the feet sideways to one shoulder-width with feet turned outward at a 45-degree angle.

NOTE: The name, *Hachiji-dachi* (eight-letter stance) comes from the Japanese character for "eight" (八).

Alternate View of Natural Stance (*Shizen-tai* or *Hachiji-dachi*) [Figure 4]

Fig. 4   The feet are one shoulder-width apart with feet turned outward at a 45-degree angle.

Section 5 – Parallel Stance (*Heiko-dachi*)

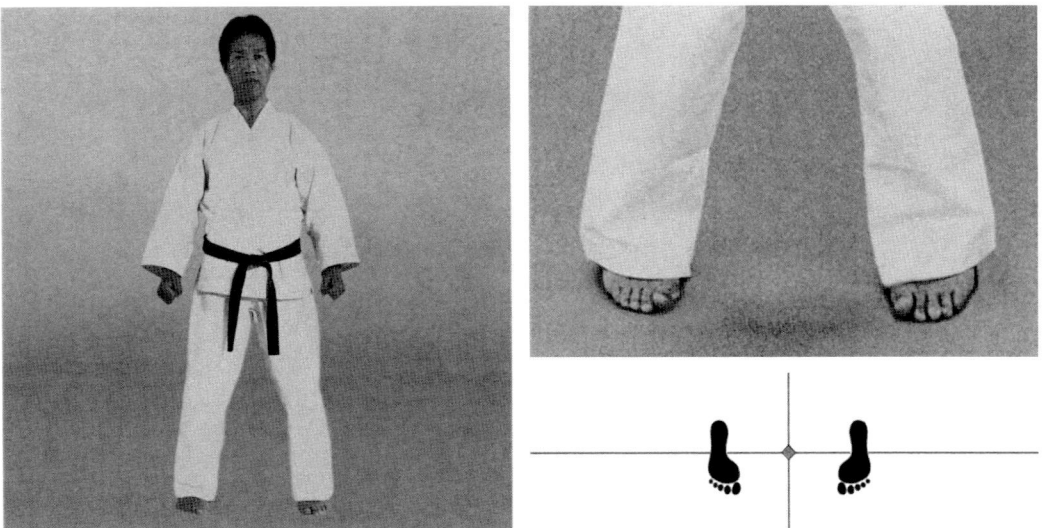

Parallel Stance (*Heiko-dachi*) [Figures 1-3]

Figs. 1-3 Place the feet in parallel with the outside edges pointing straight forward at a distance of one shoulder-width apart. The knees and shoulders are relaxed, and eyes focused forward.

Section 6 – Front Stance (*Zenkutsu-dachi*)

Front Stance (*Zenkutsu-dachi*) [Figures 1-3]

Figs. 1-3 Start with feet at shoulder-width apart and step forward to the length of approximately one and a half shoulder widths. The outer edge of the front foot points straight forward, while the back foot points approximately 45 degrees outward. The back leg is straight without locking the knee, while the front knee is bent in such a way that it rests directly above the arch of the foot (instep).

About 60 percent of the weight should be placed on the front leg with a feeling of pushing the stomach outward.

Section 7 – Straddle Stance or Horse Stance (*Kiba-dachi*)

Straddle Stance (*Kiba-dachi*) [Figures 1-3]

Figs. 1-3 Open feet one and a half shoulder-width apart, the toes tightly grasping the surface of the floor. The outer edges of the feet point straight forward. Knees are bent with their tension outward. Keep the back straight and shoulders relaxed.

Section 8 – Sumo Stance or Stamping Stance (*Shiko-dachi*)

Sumo or Stamping Stance (*Shiko-dachi*) [Figures 1-3]

Figs. 1-3   Some refer to this stance as "sumo wrestler's stance." It is formed from the straddle stance by turning both feet outward about 45 degrees (90 degrees angle to each other). The thighs are bent about 30 degrees to the shin, and the knees are directly over the ankles. back remains straight with the feeling of slightly pushing the stomach out.

Section 9 – Back Stance (*Kōkutsu-dachi*): Variations 1-2

Standard Back Stance (*Kōkutsu-dachi*): Variation One [Figures 1-3]

Figs. 1-3 Feet are perpendicular. The center line of the front foot points straight forward, while the outer edge of the back-foot points 90 degrees sideward. Approximately 70 percent of the weight should be on the back leg. Keep the back straight with power in the lower stomach (*tanden*). Front knee must be slightly bent for flexibility and balance.

Minor Back Stance (*Sho-kōtsu-dachi*): VariationTwo2 [Figures 4-6]

Figs. 4-6 Feet open to one-half the length of standard back stance. Otherwise, the execution of minor back stance is identical to standard back stance

ART AND THEORY OF SELF-DEFENSE | 63

Section 10 – Half-and-Half Stance (Modified *Fudo-dachi*)

Half-and-Half Stance (*Fudo-dachi*) [Figures 1-3]

Figs. 1-3 In standard half-and-half stance, squat down with equal weight placed on each leg and be prepared to move in any direction. The center of gravity is in the middle of the feet. The eyes should be focused on the opponent. Keep the back straight and the shoulders down and relaxed.

NOTE: This stance is a lower position of the ready-to-defend posture that can be used in the practice of various defensive techniques. However, because this is a lower stance with bent knees, it limits the agility and speed with which one can adjust their position in a self-defense situation.

Section 11 – One-Step-Forward Stance (*Moto-dachi*)

Moto-dachi is often used as a "ready-to-defend posture." Obviously, everything possible should be done to avoid a violent confrontation, but if one is in danger and cannot run away, one must defend one's self by facing the opponent with confidence, concentration and full fighting spirit. The "ready-to-defend posture" can be used in practice of defensive and preemptive techniques.

One-Step-Forward Stance (*Moto-dachi*) [Figures 1-3]

Figs. 1-3   This stance is a higher version of half-and-half stance (the knees are less bent) and often used with the fists up in "ready-to-defend posture." The stance allows for quick defensive and offensive movement. While stability and balance may be a little weaker in this higher stance, speed in self-defense is a critical factor.

Fig. 4 *Moto-dachi* is used as part of the finishing posture to represent *zan-shin*. With the downward hand position and the gaze of the eyes on the fallen attacker, the defender demonstrates "a mind that remains alert to ensure that peace is restore".

For more on *zan-shin* see Chapter 19.

Moto-dachi: *Zan-shin* Application [Figure 4]

CHAPTER 10

Strengthening the Mind-Body Connection

The premise behind the need to strengthen the mind-body connection is that *physiology creates psychology*. For an in-depth discussion of the Mind-Body Connection see Chapter 4, Section 1.

These simple exercises which harmonize the mind, body and breath can have a profound impact on individual self-development in that they increase self-awareness, self-control, and they calm and focus the mind. They can be useful as both warm-up and cool-down routines.

Section 1 – The Mind-Body Connection Exercise

A seemingly simple exercise, the mind-body connection exercise can have a profound impact on individual self-development, particularly in children. The exercise assigns a series of specific stances to certain character traits, such as respect, concentration/awareness and confidence. It must be practiced with precision and full attention in order to gain maximum benefit.

Step 1. Attention Stance = "Respect for Self"

Step 2. Bow in Attention Stance = "Respect for Others"

Step 3. Natural Stance = "Concentration"

Mind-body Connection [Steps 1-3]

Step 4. Left Front Stance = "Self-Confidence"

Step 5. Right Front Stance = "Go Forward with Self-Confidence"

Step 6. Return to Natural Stance = "Continued Concentration"

Mind-body Connection [Steps 4-6]

Step 7. Return to Attention Stance = "Never Lose Self-Respect"

Step 8. Bow in Attention Stance = "Never Lose Respect for Parents, Teachers and Peers"

Step 9. Finish in Attention Stance

Mind-body Connection [Steps 7- 9]

Section 2 – Simple Walking Exercise Joined with Breathing (*Doh-zen*)

It is important for one to sit in stillness for at least five minutes each day. Gradually, the ability to look inward will permeate daily life, and the ability to sit for longer periods will increase gradually. In time, one will see that meditation in movement (*doh-zen*) also is a valuable exercise.

Walking Exercise Joined with Breathing Practice [Figure 1]

Fig. 1 The walking exercise joined with breathing (*doh-zen*) can be performed with several different hand positions. The hand position shown, with the palms hand overlapping the left hand near the navel.

Walking Exercise Joined with Breathing Practice [Figures 2-4]

Figs. 2-4 Start in a natural stance with hands positioned near the navel. Step straight forward with the left foot and then walk naturally and slowly while concentrating on the breath.

Section 3 – *Jufu Kihon*

Jufu Kihon offers a simplified method of purposely integrating the mind, body and breath with each motion. In the practice of *Jufu Kihon*, all motions are synchronized with a steady and deep inhalation or exhalation, with complete mental focus on mind-body integration. In the practice of all *Jufu no Kata*, motions are synchronized with a steady and deep inhalation or exhalation, with complete mental focus on mind-body integration.

Jufu Kihon [Figures 1-3]

Figs. 1-3 Start in natural stance. Begin a long, complete inhalation and bring relaxed hands above the head, leading with the back of the wrists. Once the inhalation and the upward motion are complete, lower the hands downward with arms straight, palms facing each other, while the left knee is raised simultaneously to the chest. This motion coincides with a long, complete exhalation.

Jufu Kihon [Figures 4-6]

Figs. 4-6   Once the breath is fully expelled, return to natural stance, relax the hands. Begin a long, complete inhalation and bring relaxed hands above the head, leading with the back of the wrists. Once the inhalation and the upward motion are complete, lower the hands downward with arms straight, palms facing each other, while the right knee is raised simultaneously to the chest. This motion coincides with a long, complete exhalation.

Jufu Kihon [Figures 7-9]

Figs. 7-8   Begin a deep inhalation in natural stance and bring the arms above the head, beginning a large, circular motion with the arms out to the sides of the body. The inhalation and the circular motion are completed in natural stance with the hands in the position shown in Fig. 9.

Fig. 9   Once the hands are here, begin a *full, strong exhalation* and step forward with the left foot

ART AND THEORY OF SELF-DEFENSE | 73

into *moto-dachi* (see Chapter 9, Section 11: *Stances*), as the hands push forward, leading with the palm heels.

Jufu Kihon [Figures 10-11]

Figs. 10-11   Complete the exhalation at the moment the arms are straight and fully extended. Again, inhale slowly and deeply while bringing the arms above the head in a large, circular motion.

Jufu Kihon [Figures 12-13]

Figs. 12-13   Once the hands are at the sides, begin a *full, strong exhalation* and step forward to a right foot forward *moto dachi*, as the hands push forward, leading with the palm heels.

Jufu Kihon [Figures 14-16]

Figs. 14-16   As you begin inhalation, step forward with the left foot, returning to natural stance, letting the arms come to sides of the body (not shown). Take a smaller breath in, while turning your palms to face outward. Then with a smaller breath out, bring the palms to face inward as shown. Relax in natural stance.

Section 4– *Jufu no Kata Godan (Ichi)*

The dynamic, large physical movements and deep breathing of *Jufu no Kata Godan (Ichi)* assist one in maintaining continuous mental focus on this practice meditation in movement (*doh-zen*).

Jufu no Kata Godan (Ichi) [Figures 1-3]

Figs. 1-3   Start in natural stance. Begin a long, complete inhalation and bring relaxed hands above the head, leading with the back of the wrists. Once the inhalation and the upward motion are complete, slide the left foot sideways to sumo, or stamping stance (see Chapter 9: *Stances*). Begin a long, complete exhalation in unison with the downward motion of the hands, leading with the palm heels. Hands maintain a softness as they move, pushing with the palm heels.

Jufu no Kata Godan (Ichi) [Figures 4-6]

Figs. 4-5   Upon completing the exhalation, relax the hands. Begin a full inhalation and bring relaxed hands above the head leading with the back of the wrists. At the finish of the inhalation, slide the left foot back to natural stance.

Fig. 6   Momentarily, hold the breath to adjust left foot to left front stance with arms above the head.

Jufu no Kata Godan (Ichi) **[Figures 7-9]**

Figs. 7-8 Begin a long, complete exhalation, gradually bring the arms down, leading with the palm heels and lower the torso forward over the left thigh, allowing the arms to go all way up, above the back. Complete the exhalation fully—expelling every bit of air.

Fig. 9 Begin to inhale and gradually bring your relaxed hands up, the way they came, leading with the back of the wrists, while lifting the torso upward. Complete the inhalation with the hands above the head, not shown (similarly to above Fig. 6).

Momentarily hold the breath, while adjusting the left foot toward the front to a transitional natural stance with the arms overhead. (Transition not shown)

Jufu no Kata Godan (Ichi) **[Figures 10-12]**

Fig. 10 Then adjust the right foot into a right front stance.

Figs. 11-12 Begin a long, complete exhalation, gradually bring the arms down, leading with the palm heels, while lowering the torso forward over the right thigh. Allow the arms to go all way up above the back. Complete the exhalation fully—expelling every bit of air.

Jufu no Kata Godan (Ichi) **[Figures 13-15]**

Fig. 13 Begin inhalation. Adjust the right foot to the front while lifting the arms up, hands relaxed and leading with the back of the wrists. This is a transitional motion.

Figs. 14-15   Return to natural stance, finish the inhalation with arms above the head. Begin a long, complete exhalation and slide the left foot sideways into sumo, or stamping stance (see Chapter 9: *Stances*). Simultaneously, begin a downward motion with the hands, leading with the palm heels. Complete exhalation.

Jufu no Kata Godan (Ichi) **[Figures 16-18]**

Fig. 16 Begin a deep inhalation. Return to natural stance by sliding the left foot in and bringing the arms above the head, as shown, crossing the left hand on top of the right. This starts a large, circular motion with the arms out to the sides of the body (not shown). The inhalation and the circular motion are completed in natural stance with the hands in the position shown in Fig. 17.

Figs. 17-18   Once the hands are here, begin a *full, strong exhalation* and step forward with the right foot into *moto dachi*. Push the hands forward, leading with the palm heels. Complete the exhalation when the arms are straight and fully extended. Arm position in Fig. 18 is before the full extension.

Jufu no Kata Godan (Ichi) **[Figures 19-21]**

As you begin inhalation, step forward with the left foot, returning to natural stance, letting the arms come to sides of the body. (Not shown)

Figs. 19-21 Take a smaller breath in, while turning your palms to face outward. Then with a smaller breath out, bring the palms to face inward as shown. Relax in natural stance.

CHAPTER 11

The Fist

In the teaching of self-defense, it is important to choose the correct language when presenting the punching and striking techniques, as these are used solely for defensive maneuvers. When one teaches children how to make a fist and refers to the fist as a *self-defense fist*, then the message of the ethical principle of non-violence is immediately communicated. Further, it opens the discussion to remind students of the importance of not misusing a punch or strike to demonstrate one's skill or to start a fight.

Section 1 – Self-power (*Ji-riki*): The Significance of the Fist in the Mind-Body Connection

Learning to make a correct fist and to execute a correct punch can be a very empowering lesson for an individual, particularly for those who lack confidence. The deliberate step-by-step process of making a fist offers an experience of *ji-riki* (one's own strength). It can be practiced as follows:

(1) Fully open the hand by extending the fingers.
(2) Roll the four fingers into the palm, starting with the small finger.
(3) Then fully tighten the small figure to support the three larger fingers and wrap the thumb.
(4) Extend the arm forward and flatten the wrist to align the top of the "fisted" hand with the top of the forearm.

Making a strong fist which is staged to make a defensive strike offers an experience of inner strength to one who is in a hopeless situation and unable to feel safe. The internal message might be: "I can hold my ground, make decisions and act in a way to protect myself."

Section 2 – Making the Traditional Fist or Fore Fist: Two Methods

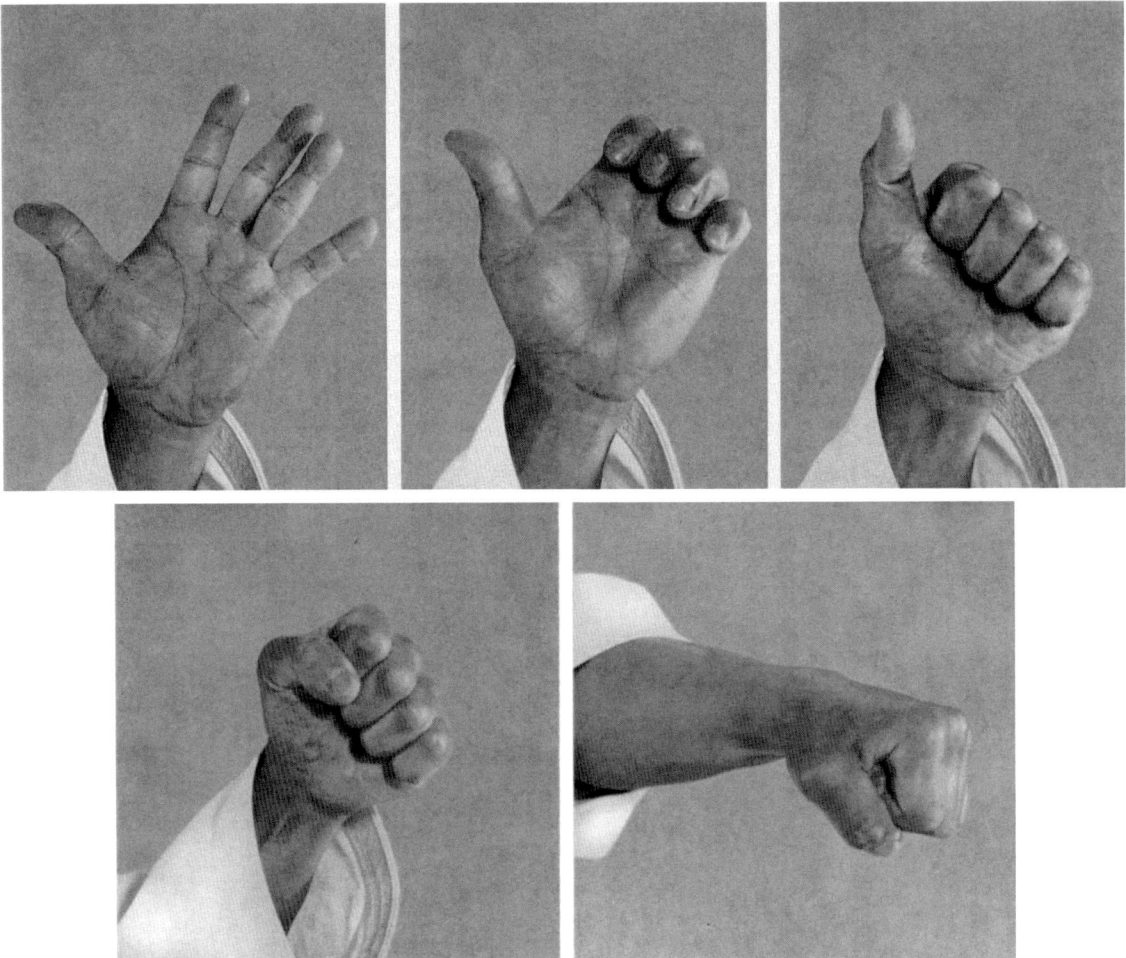

Traditional Fist: Method One [Figures 1-5]

Fig. 1   Open the hand fully to prepare to make a fist.

Fig. 2   Bend the first and the second joints of all four fingers, consecutively beginning with the small finger and ending with the index finger.

Fig. 3   Curl the fingertips into the palm firmly, making sure that the little finger does not become weak.

Fig. 4   Bend the thumb to cover the curled index finger.

Fig. 5   Keep the back of the wrists straight. The point of contact on the target consists mainly of the first two knuckles.

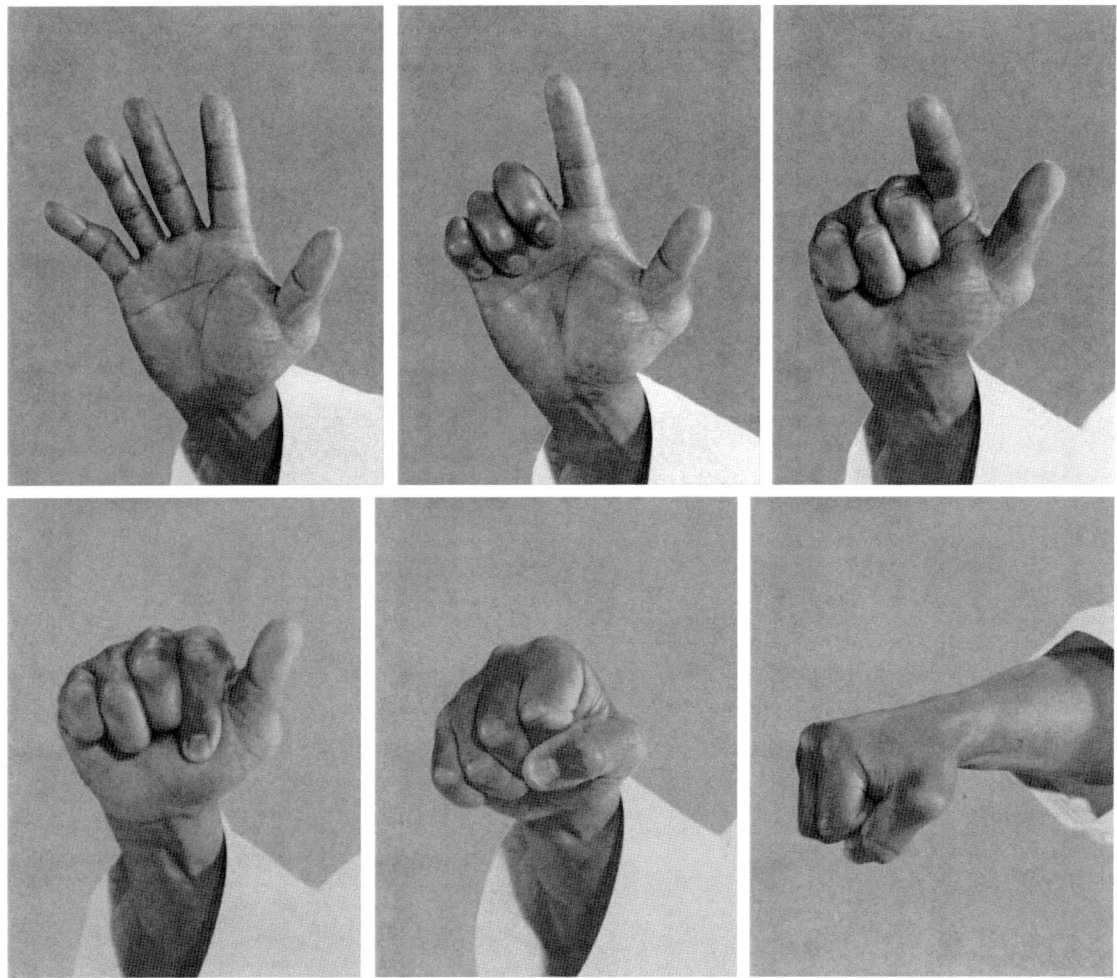

Traditional Fist: Method Two [Figures 1-6]

Fig. 1   Open the hand fully to prepare to make a fist.

Figs. 2-3 Bend the first and the second joints of the last three fingers, consecutively, beginning with the small finger.

Fig. 4   Bend only the second joint of the index finger. Curl the fingertips into the palm firmly, making sure that the little finger does not become weak.

Fig. 5   Bend the thumb and tuck it over the index finger.

Fig. 6   Keep the back of the wrists straight. The point of contact on the target consists mainly of the first two knuckles.

NOTE: The fist should be securely formed, but it should not be tight. At the moment of execution of the punch, the fist tightens primarily at the small finger and then immediately relaxes.

CHAPTER 12

Striking Surfaces and Striking Targets
Positioning and Targeting the Hands and Feet in Self-Defense

Striking Surfaces

An underlying principle of empty-hand self-defense techniques, which have been developed over centuries of study, is to make the body itself an effective "weapon" for defense. We consider 20 striking surfaces on the hands, arms, feet, and legs which best serve as surface points for delivering the power of a strike, whether as a defensive move (block) or an offensive move (counterattack). Correct formation of the various hand and foot positions is essential.

Striking Targets (Vital Points)

The following diagram of striking targets is presented primarily for academic purposes. In any dangerous self-defense situation, basic knowledge of the vital points could be life-saving. However, it must be emphasized that at this basic level of self-defense education, it is extremely important to remember the highest and most effective training of true defense is *prevention*—avoidance of any possible confrontation.

Many vital points of the human body are located on the mid-line, which is known as *seichū-sen*. Therefore, when practicing a punch, for example, it's important to focus on *seichū-sen* (imaginary mid-line). Then, in a real situation, one will find that it is more instinctive to hit a vital target, if forced to do so. Striking the outer and auxiliary targets can seriously injure an attacker. They are very useful as targets for "stunning techniques" which may temporarily stop the aggressor and allow one to escape.

Section 1 – Striking Surfaces of the Hands

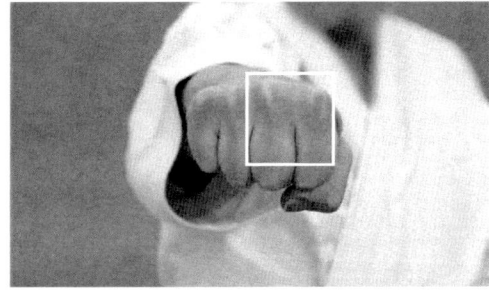

Image 1: Fore Fist (*Seiken*)

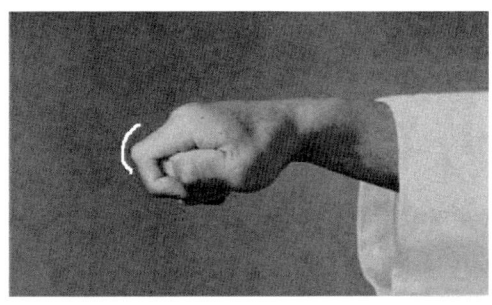

Image 2: One-Knuckle Fist (*Ippon-ken*)

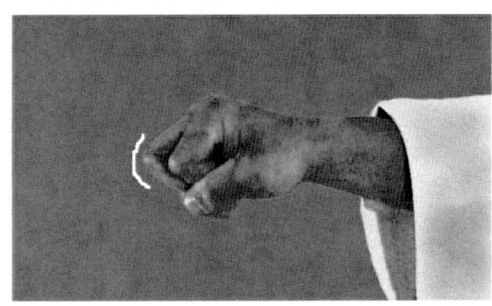

Image 3: Middle One-Knuckle Fist (*Nakadate-ippon-ken*)

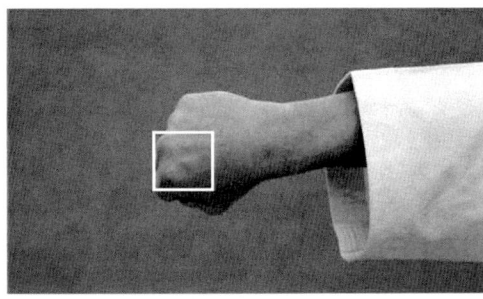

Image 4: Back Fist (*Uraken*)

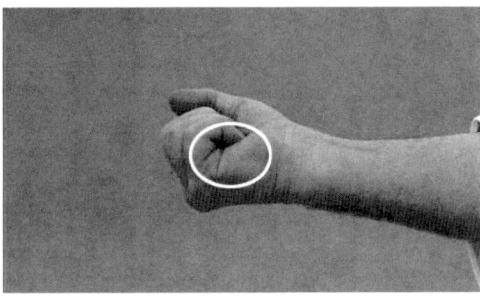

Image 5: Hammer Fist (*Tettsui*)

Striking Surfaces of the Hands [Images 1-5]

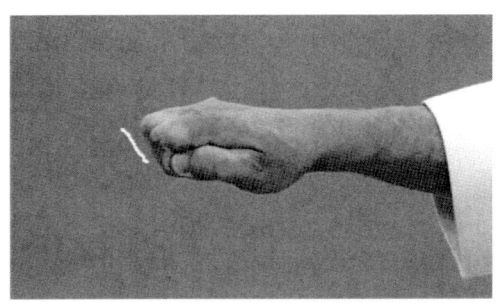

Image 6: Fore-Knuckle or Flat Fist (*Hiraken*)

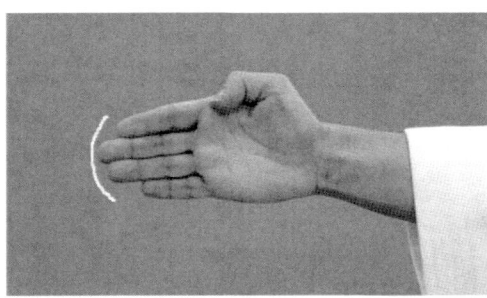

Image 7: Spear Hand (*Nukite*)

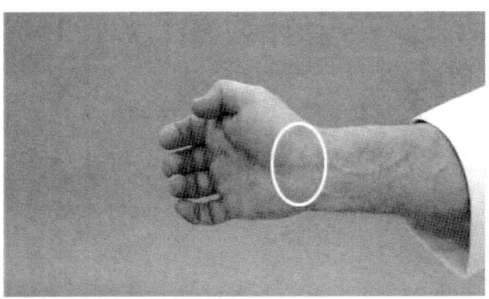

Image 8: Palm Heel (*Teisho*)

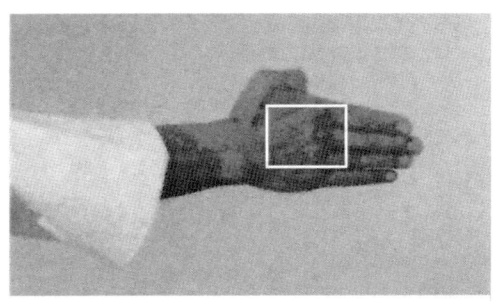

Image 9: Back Hand (*Haishu*)

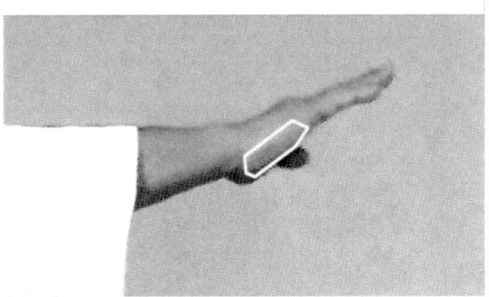

Image 10: Knife Hand (*Shuto*)

Striking Surfaces of the Hands [Images 6-10]

ART AND THEORY OF SELF-DEFENSE | 87

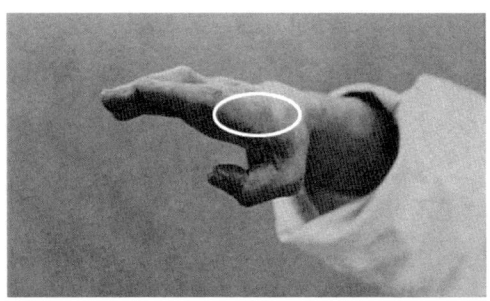

Image 11: Ridge Hand (*Haito*)

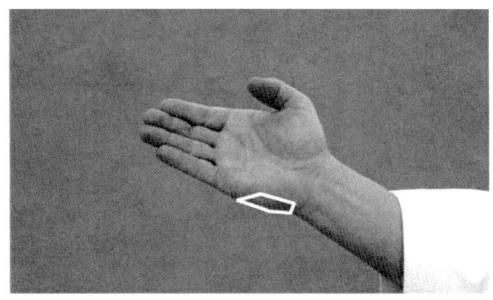

Image 12: Ox-Jaw Hand or Blue Dragon (*Seiryuto*)

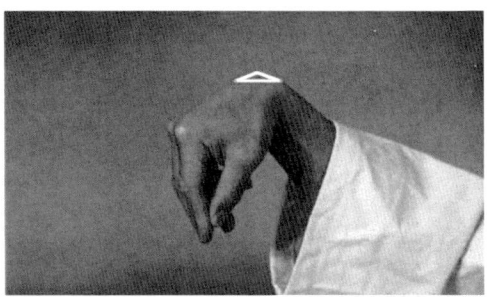

Image 13: Bent Wrist (*Kakuto Koken*)

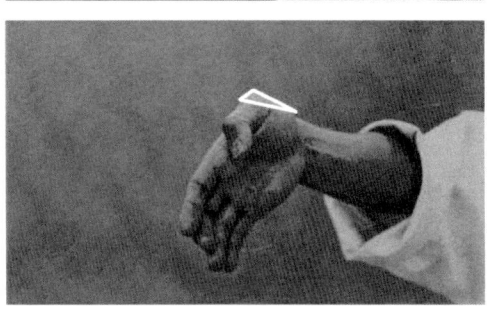

Image 14: Chicken-Head Wrist (*Keito*)

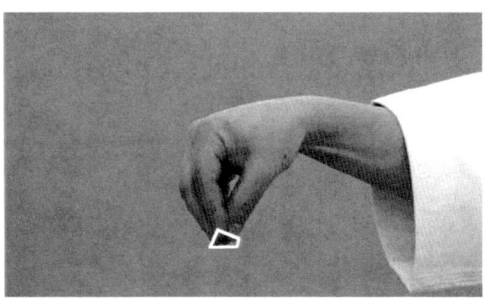

Image 15: Eagle Beak (*Washide*)

Striking Surfaces of the Hands [Images 11-15]

Section 2 – Striking Surfaces of the Feet

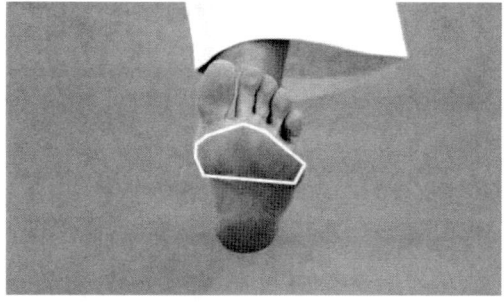

Image 16: Ball of the Foot (*Koshi*)

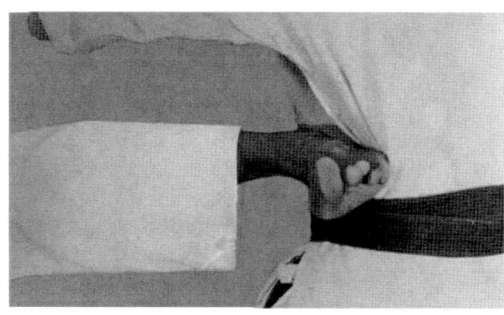

Image 17: Foot Edge or Blade (*Sokuto*)

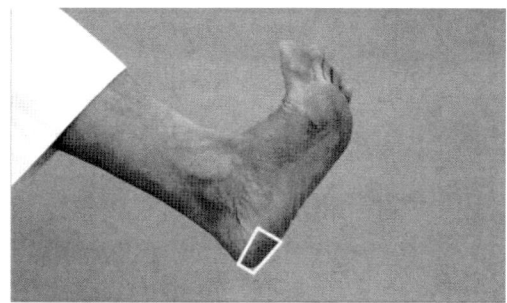

Image 18: Heel of the Foot (*Kakato*)

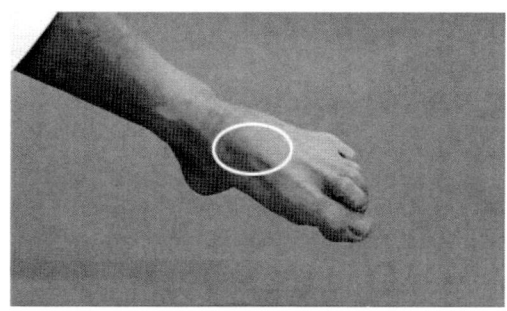

Image 19: Instep of the Foot (*Haisoku*)

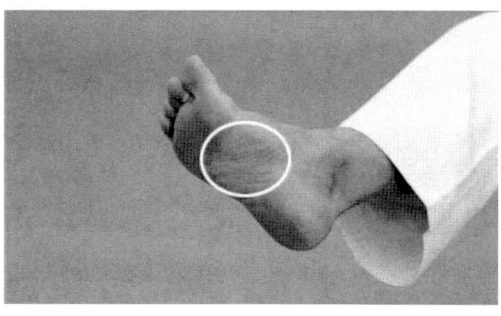

Image 20: Sole of the Foot (*Teisoku*)

Striking Surfaces of the Feet [Images 16-20]

Section 3 – Striking Targets: Front of the Human Body

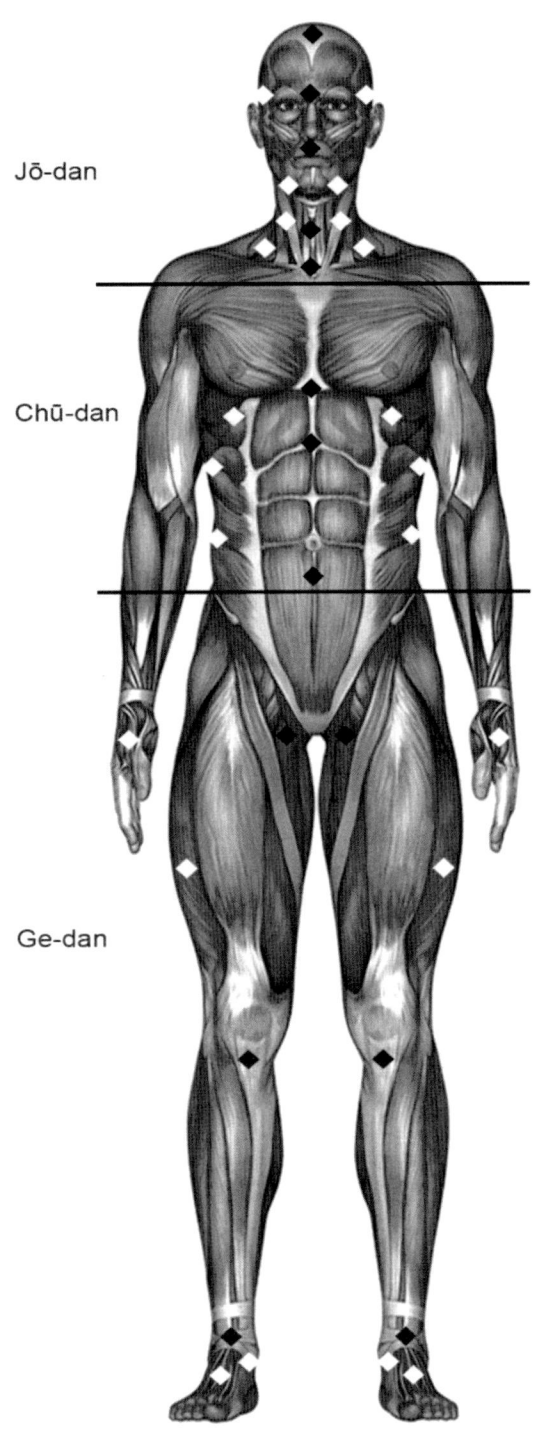

Jō-dan (High Level) Targets

1. Frontal Fontanel: joint of frontal/parietal skull bones
2. Temples
3. Glabella: top of bridge of nose
4. Eyeballs and Circumorbital structure (not shown)
5. Philtrum: space between nose and upper lip
6. Side Lower Jaw or Mandible: 1 of 3 striking points, also front of chin & upper mandible, below ear, are targets
7. Neck: most superficial and the largest muscles in the front of the neck are the targets
8. Adam's Apple (laryngeal protuberance)
9. Hollow above collar bones (supraclavicular fossa)
10. Hollow at pit of throat (suprasternal notch)

Chū-dan (Middle Level) Targets

1. Xiphoid process: the lowest section of the sternum, just above the solar plexus. Also, the sternal angle, at the top of the body of the sternum between the upper pectoral muscles is a target.
2. Solar plexus: soft center of chest just below the sternum
3. Point about one inch below the umbilicus
4. Chest area below nipples: Space between 4th & 5th ribs
5. Abdomen at 7th intercostal space on either side
6. Abdomen at 11h intercostal space (floating rib)

Ge-dan (Lower Level) Targets

1. Groin: Inguinal region on either side on males
2. Hand: hollow area between the thumb and index fingers
3. Lower Lateral Thigh: lateral vastus muscle
4. Patellar tendon: 1 of 3 striking points on the shin, with another located in the middle front of the shin (not shown)
5. Fibular notch: 3rd target on shin where tibia joins ankle
6. Inner Ankle (medial malleolus): the bony bump on inner ankle at attachment of deltoid ligament
7. Instep

Section 4 – Striking Targets: Back of the Human Body

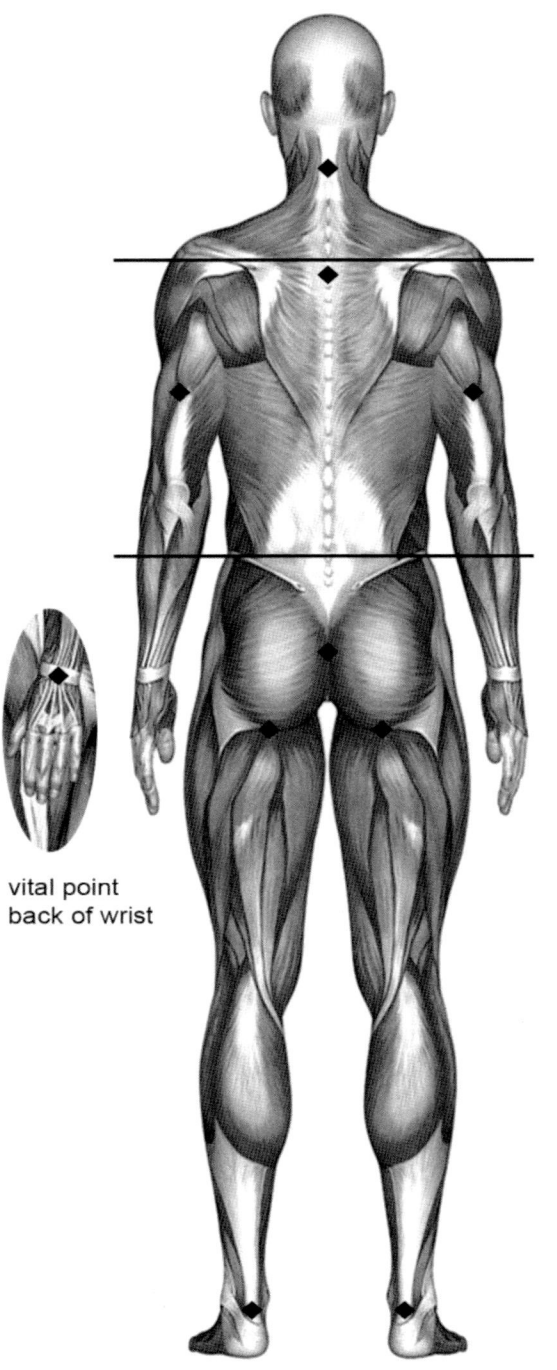

vital point
back of wrist

Jō-dan (High Level) Targets

1. Coronal Suture: middle of the top of the head (not marked)
2. Back of the Neck at the 3rd intervertebral space

Chū-dan (Middle Level) Targets

1. Spine a level of 3rd intercostal space: on line with scapular ridge, middle
2. Upper arm: dorsal surface at the intersection of the biceps and triceps

Ge-dan (Lower Level) Targets

1. Back of the Wrist: space between the lower ends of the radius and ulna
2. Spinal Tip (Tailbone)
3. Gluteal fold: center of the most upper thigh just below the buttocks
4. Achilles tendon

CHAPTER 13

Blocking

Traditionally, blocking techniques are regarded as more important than attacking techniques. Ideally, a student of self-defense should be able to block or dodge the attacks of their opponent(s) without resorting to counterattacks. For this reason, emphasis must be placed on precision, timing and speed in blocking techniques. Powerful blocking technique is developed through precise, concentrated training.

Section 1 – Upper Block (*Age-uke*)

Upper Block (*Age-uke*) [Figures 1-2]

Fig. 1 Assume natural stance and bring the right arm above the forehead with an open hand as shown and place left fist palm up at the hip.

Fig. 2 Start to move the left arm out keeping elbow close to the body and pointing downward with the feeling of aiming the left hand at something toward the right shoulder.

Upper Block (*Age-uke*) [Figures 3-4]

Fig. 3   Continue to move the left arm across the chest and under the right arm with the left fist crossing at the throat. Do not twist the left fist until the end of the technique.

Fig. 4   At the moment of execution, twist the forearm so that the palm-side of the fist faces outward. The twisting motion gives power to the blocking arm. The elbow should be bent about 120 degrees, and the forearm should be positioned above the forehead with its palm side facing the attacker. Do not try to scoop the attacking arm; rather, try to deflect the attack with the correct method.

Example of Application of Upper Block [Figure 5]

Fig. 5   A proper upper block is effective against an attacker's upper punch.

Section 2 – Middle Striking Block (*Uchi-uke*)

Middle Striking Block (*Uchi-uke*) [Figures 1-2]

Fig. 1   Bring the left arm to the ready-to-block position with the palm side of the hand facing down.

Fig. 2   Without changing the face of the left fist, bring it to the midsection. Do not drop the elbow yet.

Middle Striking Block (*Uchi-uke*) [Figures 3-4]

Fig. 3   At the moment of blocking, twist the fist so that its palm side faces upward. Simultaneously drop the elbow downward to complete the block.

Fig. 4   Make sure that the elbow of the blocking arm does not extend too far out from the body.

Section 3 – Middle Inside/Outside Block (*Soto-uke*)

Middle Inside/Outside Block (*Soto-uke*) [Figures 1-2]

Figs. 1-2 Cross arms in front of the chest with the blocking arm placed under the other. Fists both have their palm sides downward at this point. Then, bring the blocking arm across the chest with its elbow as the pivotal center of the movement. The pulling arm should slide on the inside of the elbow of the blocking arm as it is being brought back to the hip.

Middle Inside/Outside Block (*Soto-uke*) [Figures 1-2]

Fig. 3-4   At the moment of the block, the palm sides of both fists face upward with the elbow pointing down and the fist of the blocking arm should be positioned at the shoulder level, slightly beyond the line of the elbow in the end. In executing this block, make contact with the attacking arm as if scooping from below and then pushing sideward and outward with the fist. Thus, the fist of blocking arm twists in such a way, that it ends up slightly over the top of the attacking arm.

Section 4 – Down or Downward Block (*Gedan-barai*)

Downward Block (*Gedan-barai*) [Figures 1-2]

Fig. 1   If the right arm is the blocking arm, bring the right fist to the left shoulder with its palm facing upward and pinky side of the fist on the shoulder.

Fig. 2   The blocking arm slides over the pulling arm. Keep the palm side of the blocking arm's fist facing upward.

Downward Block (*Gedan-barai*) [Figures 3-4]

Fig. 3   At the moment of the block, turn the fist of the blocking arm so that its palm side faces downward.

Fig. 4   This blocking technique can be applied against a middle punch.

Downward Block (*Gedan-barai*) [Figure 5]

Fig. 5   Shown is a left downward block.

Section 5 – Wedge Block (*Kakiwake-uke*)

Wedge Block (*Kakiwake-uke*) [Figures 1-2]

Fig. 1   Cross the arms in front of the chest with the palm side of the fists towards the face.

Fig. 2   As the block is executed, turn the fists so the palm side of the fists face out and bring the elbows down slightly and closer to the body.

Wedge Block (*Kakiwake-uke*) Application [Figure 3]

Fig. 3   Use this block against an attacker who is attempting to choke or grab the neck. Drop the hips down and back as the arms make contact with the attacking arms.

Section 6 – Cross Block or X-Block: Upward and Downward (*Juji-uke*)

Upward and Downward Cross Block (*Juji-uke*) [Figures 1-3]

Fig. 1 In preparation, place both hands at the hips as in the ready position for punching.

Fig. 2 In the upper-cross block, bring both arms straight, crossing at the wrists, to block an attack above the forehead with the right arm on the inside, closest to the head.

Fig. 3 In downward-cross block, bring the crossed arms down from the sides of the hips.

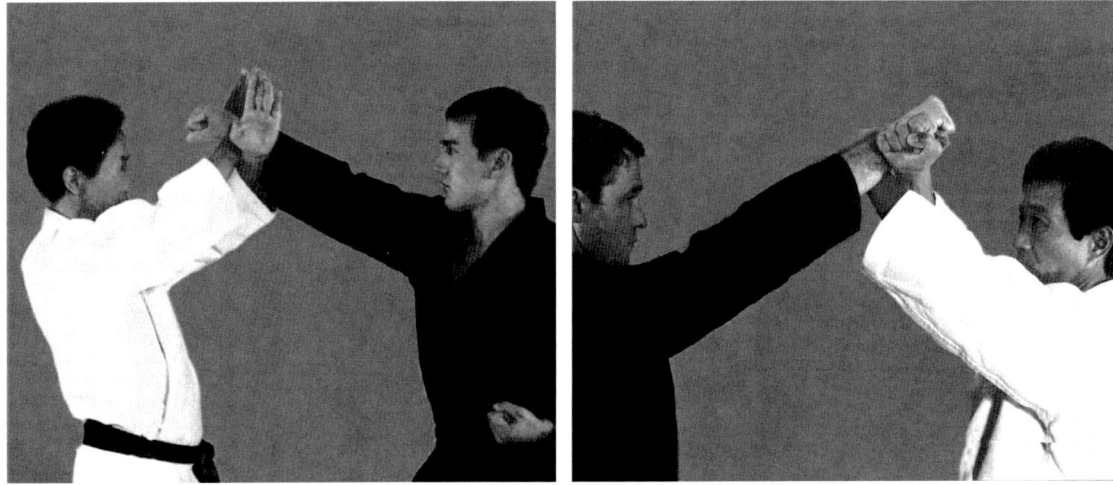

Upward Cross Block (*Juji-uke*) Application [Figures 4-5]

Figs. 4-5 At the moment of the block, press the crossed hands against each other at the wrists, catching and pushing the attacking arm up. It is primarily used for blocking an attacker's forearm. The upward cross block can be executed with either fists or open hands.

Upward Cross Block (*Juji-uke*) to Back-Fist Strike [Figures 6-7]

Fig. 6   Execute an upward cross block against the attacker's right arm overhead strike.

Fig. 7   Grab the attacker's right arm with the left hand and execute a right back-fist to the attacker's philtrum (shown), temple or bridge of nose.

Note: While this chapter emphasizes blocking without the use of counterattack, the upper cross block is often followed by a grab and strike (shown). The lower cross block is often followed by a throw (not shown).

Downward Cross Block (*Juji-uke*) Application [Figures 8-9]

Figs. 8-9   The downward cross block can also be executed with either fists or open hands and is used against a middle punch or front kick.

ART AND THEORY OF SELF-DEFENSE | 101

Section 7 – Scooping Block (*Sukui-uke*)

Scooping Block (*Sukui-uke*) [Figures 1-3]

Fig. 1   In preparation, bring the blocking arm above the shoulder with the palm side of the fist facing away from the body.

Figs. 2-3   Swing the blocking arm down, making an arc toward the target. At the moment the arm is blocking, twist the fist so that it turns to face palm side up.

Scooping Block Application [Figures 4-5]

Fig. 4   To make this block effective, twist the hip toward the blocking arm.

Fig. 5   This rotation of the hip can be achieved with or without adjusting the stance. If the stance changes and the blocking arm is the right arm, step back with the left foot at the moment of the block. This technique will break the attacker's balance and allow for counterattack by either throwing or punching.

Section 8 – Open Hand Half-Circle Block (*Kaisho Han-en-uke*)

Open Hand Half-Circle Block (*Kaisho Han-en-uke*) with Palm heel Strike to Chin [Figures 1-3]

Figs. 1-3 Using the right hand with open palm facing away, start from lower inside and make a clockwise circular motion, blocking the upper region of the body, head and neck.

Open Hand Half-Circle Block (*Kaisho Han-en-uke*) with Palm heel Strike to Chin [Figures 4-6]

Figs. 4-6 Once the block is completed, prepare and execute a right palm heel strike.

Section 9 – Knee Block (*Hiza-uke*)

Knee Block (*Hiza-uke*) [Figures 1-3]

Fig. 1 Assume the ready-to-defend position.

Fig. 2 Bring the blocking knee high in the ready position.

Fig. 3 Bring the knee in a roundhouse motion towards the target.

Knee Block (*Hiza-uke*) Application [Figure 4]

Fig. 4 This block can be used as a block against a punch or a kick.

CHAPTER 14

Punching and Striking
The Use of Hands and Arms in Self-Defense

Human hands and elbows are natural weapons for self-defense. The fisted hand in a traditional punch is the primary defensive tool. In self-defense, the punch is practiced in such a way as to provide maximum defensive benefit with a single blow. Other than the traditional punch, this book outlines methods of using the fisted hand to adapt to the many possible circumstances that can arise in self-defense. For example, the hook punch and the non-twisting punch are best used within fighting situations when the attacker is very close.

When self-defense punches are executed, the hips, legs and trunk must move simultaneously to complete the technique effectively. Speed and the use of *tanden* (see Chapter 7, Section 4: *Tanden*) are also important in producing an effective punch. As in all self-defense technique, the *tanden* plays an important role.

Punching stands alone in the arena of striking with the hands and arms, because by definition a punch is a fisted hand that derives its power by the linear alignment of the wrist, forearm and elbow directly behind it. Two examples of a fisted hand techniques which are not punches are the hammer fist strike and back-fist strike. The spear hand strike is a variation of the straight punch, but is not identified as such, in that the hand is not in a fisted position.

Use of the arms or hands, whether fisted or not, which do not comply with the definition of a punch, are called "strikes."

Section 1 – Practice of Punching and Important Elements of a Correct Punch

A. The punching hand should travel the shortest distance to the target, which is a straight line between the starting point and the target. It is important to rub the elbow of the punching arm against the side of the body. In a well-formed punch, the elbow will remain behind the fist in direct alignment, following the path of the fist exactly.

B. The shoulders must be kept relaxed at all times, feeling power in the lower abdomen (*tanden*), keeping the elbow close to the body to engage the latissimus dorsi muscle. The size and location of this muscle makes it a critical muscle to executing a correct punch. Ultimately, the latissimus dorsi muscle connects the power of the hips and legs to the punching motion. At the instant that the punch is executed, all the muscles should be momentarily tensed, including those in the chest and in the back.

C. The pulling arm and punching arm must be synchronized, emphasizing the action-reaction principle. Snapping the arm increases the speed of the punch and makes the muscles in the abdomen and arm tense at the moment of impact. Twisting the arm, as it moves, adds to the force and ensures that the direction of the force is stable.

D. Speed is important in self-defense technique. A simple but important principle applied in self-defense is power equals mass times acceleration times velocity (P = m *x* a *x* v). The principle implies that power can transcend the size of the defender through the application of correct techniques. In other words, it is possible for a small person to produce a greater power than a larger person by applying more velocity as he or she executes the technique.

E. Another principle behind executing an effective self-defense punch is to centralize the force of the punch to a vital point on the body. Many vital points of the human body are located on the mid-line, which is known as *seichū-sen*. Therefore, when practicing a punch, it's important to focus on *seichū-sen* (imaginary mid-line).

Application: Traditional Punch with a Middle One-Knuckle Fist (*Nakadate-ippon-ken*) to Solar Plexus

Section 2 – Traditional Punch: Fore-fist Straight Punch (*Seiken-choku-zuki*)

Fig. 1 Begin in natural stance. Relax the shoulders and body. Place the punching hand (the right) just above the hipbone with its palm side up. Extend the pulling arm (the left) straight in front. The pulling hand (left) is important in self-defense punching because the basic principle of action-reaction must be applied in executing punches. Do not twist the punching fist too early. Wait until the elbow passes the body.

Fig. 2 Push the punching hand out straight, with its elbow rubbing the side of the body, thus making sure that the fist travels the shortest route to the target by following a straight line.

Fig. 3 As the elbow passes beyond the side of the body, the punching arm twists inward and straightens at the point of full extension. Simultaneously, the pulling arm retracts and twists to ready position with palm up at the top of the hip. Relax the shoulders at all times. Try to synchronize the two arms – punching and pulling.

Traditional Punch (*Seiken-choku-zuki*)
Front View [Figures 1-3]

Fig. 1 Begin in natural stance. Relax the shoulders and body. Place the punching hand (right) just above the hipbone with its palm side up. Extend the pulling arm (left) straight in front. The pulling hand (left) is important in self-defense punching because the basic principle of action-reaction must be applied in executing punches. Do not twist the punching fist too early. Wait until the elbow passes the body.

Fig. 2 Push the punching hand out straight, with its elbow rubbing the side of the body, thus making sure that the fist travels the shortest route to the target by following a straight line.

Fig. 3 As the elbow passes beyond the side of the body, the punching arm twists inward and straightens at the point of full extension. Simultaneously, the pulling arm retracts and twists to ready position with palm up at the top of the hip. Relax the shoulders at all times. Try to synchronize the two arms – punching and pulling.

Traditional Punch (*Seiken-choku-zuki*)
Side View [Figures 1-3]

Section 3 – Traditional Punch in Front Stance: Lunge Punch (*Oi-zuki*) and Reverse Punch (*Gyaku-zuki*)

Lunge Punch (*Oi-zuki*) [Figure 1]

Reverse Punch (*Gyaku-zuki*) [Figure 2]

Fig. 1   From natural stance, lunge forward with the left foot and execute a left middle punch. Keep the back straight and the rear foot fully on the floor. As the punching arm moves forward, the hips rotate slightly to follow the direction of the punch, and the shoulders remain down and relaxed. At the moment of impact, the arm should be fully extended and muscles tightened with the hips rotated to maximize the force and extension of the punch.

Fig. 2   Execute the punch with the opposite hand of the leg in a front stance. As shown, the left leg is forward and the punch is executed with the right arm.

NOTE: Either punch can be executed as an upper punch or middle punch. The upper punch focuses on the face or throat of the attacker. The middle focuses on the solar plexus or ribs.

Application: Traditional Punch with a Vertical Fist (*Tate-ken*) to Floating Rib

Section 4 – Practice of Striking

Though, technically, all striking can be practiced as stand-alone techniques, it is important to remember the ethical principle behind all self-defense practice which is: there is no strike without an attack first. Therefore, when practicing striking techniques, it is important to precede the practice of the strike with some sort of defensive technique. For example, in the practice of elbow strikes, begin with a block and follow with the elbow strike.

Section 5 – Back-Fist Strike (*Ura-Ken Uchi*)

While not as powerful as a standard straight punch, the standard back-fist strike can be very useful in self-defense situations because of the speed with which it is delivered. Back-fist strikes are primarily used to target the upper portion of the body from the head to the solar plexus. The power in the back-fist originates from the snapping motion executed from the elbow to the wrist, as if using the arm as a whip. Because of the back-fist's relative lack of power, it is most effective when used on vital points of the attacker's body, such as the temple, bridge of the nose, philtrum or solar plexus.

During execution of a back-fist, the practitioner will find more velocity is achieved in the whipping technique if the mind is focused on a swift and complete pull-back motion. In certain instances, both hands can execute the snapping back-fist strike simultaneously. In a properly executed snapping back-fist technique, impact is made with the back of the first two knuckles of the fist. There are three primary types of snapping back-fist: side, reverse and downward.

SIDE BACK-FIST STRIKE

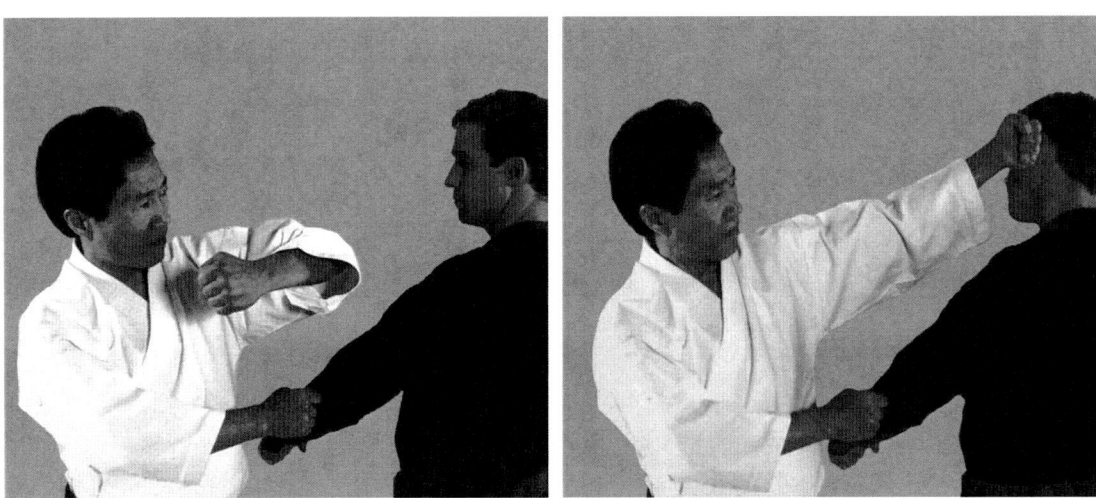

Side Back-Fist Strike (*Ura-ken Uchi*) [Figures 1-2]

Figs. 1-2 Fully bend the elbow of the striking arm, then snap the arm sideways at the elbow and strike at the attacker's temple with the sideways back-fist, emphasizing the quick pull back (not shown).

REVERSE SIDE BACK-FIST STRIKE

Reverse Side Back-Fist Strike [Figures 3-4]

Figs. 3-4 Begin with the fist of the striking arm positioned with the palm side up. As the fist twists, the palm side turns away from the target and strikes the temple.

DOWNWARD BACK-FIST STRIKE

Downward Back-Fist Strike [Figures 5-6]

Figs. 5-6 Begin with the fist turned so that its palm faces the attacker. Attack the bridge of the attacker's nose (or philtrum) with the back-fist strike, twisting the fist at the moment of striking.

Section 6 – Elbow Strikes (*Empi-uchi*)

The hard and pointed surface of the elbow can be an effective self-defense weapon. Elbow strikes are useful in self-defense when one is in close proximity to the attacker. An elbow strike is used as "stunning technique" to disable an opponent, or it can be applied as a "finishing technique" when accurately targeting a vital point on the attacker's body.

UPPER ELBOW STRIKE (THREE VIEWS)

Upper Elbow Strike (*Empi-uchi*) – Side View [Figures 1-3]

Figs. 1-2 From natural stance step the left foot forward and raise the arm into a left upper block position with the palm open. Then, move the right fist out from the hip with the palm facing upward (as if to punch).

Fig. 3 Continue raising the arm with the elbow bent. As the upper arm passes shoulder level, rapidly thrust the elbow upward and twist the palm of the fist to face the ear.

Upper Elbow Strike (*Empi-uchi*) – Front View [Figures 4-6]

Upper Elbow Strike (*Empi-uchi*) – Top View [Figures 7-9]

SIDE ELBOW STRIKE (TWO VIEWS)

Side Elbow Strike (*Empi-uchi*) Front View [Figures 1-3]

Fig. 1   In straddle stance, place the right fist, palm side up, on the left shoulder.

Fig. 2   Pull the fist across the center of the chest toward the right side of the body, with the palm still facing up.

Fig. 3   To begin to execute the side elbow strike, slide sideways in straddle stance and at the moment of striking, twist the right fist palm downward and pull the left fist to the hip.

Side Elbow Strike (*Empi-uchi*) Top View [Figures 4-5]

BACK ELBOW STRIKE (TWO VIEWS)

Back Elbow Strike (*Empi-uchi*) Side View [Figures 1-3]

Fig.1 In natural stance, the fist of the striking arm is outstretched with the palm facing downward. Left hand is on the hip.

Fig. 2 Stepping back with the right foot, pull the striking hand back to the right hip and twist the fist so the palm side ends upward. This motion follows the path of retracting a hand from a front middle-punch.

Fig 3 At the moment of striking, the open hand of the left arm is aligned approximately one fist-height above the right fist.

Back Elbow Strike (*Empi-uchi*) Front View [Figures 4-6]

FRONT ELBOW STRIKE (TWO VIEWS)

Front Elbow Strike (*Empi-uchi*) Side View [Figures 1-3]

Fig. 1   From natural stance step the left foot forward and raise the left arm straight out with the left hand extended with the palm open and facing down.

Fig. 2   Beginning to execute the front elbow strike, move the right arm out with the palm facing upward (as if to punch) and begin pulling the left arm backward to the hip.

Fig. 3   To complete the front elbow strike, thrust the elbow forward while keeping the forearm parallel to the floor. Quickly twist the palm of the fist downward.

Front Elbow Strike (*Empi-uchi*) Front View [Figures 4-6]

DOWNWARD ELBOW STRIKE

Downward Elbow Strike (*Empi-uchi*) [Figures 1-3]

Fig. 1   Begin in natural stance. In preparation for the downward strike, extend the left arm (pulling arm) in front at the height of the left hip and step back with the right foot. Raise the striking arm above the head with its fist turned so that the palm is facing outward.

Fig. 2   Quickly snap the elbow downward and, at the moment of execution, twist the forearm inward allowing the fist to turn with the palm side facing the shoulder.

Fig. 3   This strike can also be finished in a kneeling position with the right knee down.

Application of Downward Elbow Strike (*Empi-uchi*) to Collar Bone from Standing Position [Figures 4-6]

Figs. 4-6   Attacker attempts a grab to the throat, defender executes an upper wedge block in natural stance. Defender grabs the attacker's right arm and then pulls it to his left hip, while simultaneously preparing for a downward elbow strike with the right arm (palm of fist facing away). At the moment of execution, the forearm twists counterclockwise allowing the fist to turn inward.

Section 7 – Application of Elbow Strikes

UPPER ELBOW STRIKE—APPLICATION

Upper Elbow Strike (*Empi-uchi*) Application [Figures 1-2]

Fig. 1   From the natural stance, block the attacker's right upper lunge punch with a left upper block.

Fig. 2   Grab the attacker's arm with the blocking arm. Step in with the right foot to prepare for an upper elbow strike.

Upper Elbow Strike (*Empi-uchi*) Application [Figures 3-4]

Figs. 3-4   Bring the attacker's attacking arm close to the left hip and move right arm in an upward motion to execute the upper elbow strike, as if hitting attacker's jaw with the elbow. The palm of the striking arm is near the ear and should face the right temple at the completion of the technique.

NOTE: The upper elbow strike can be executed to the attacker's midsection (solar plexus) as well. *Practice safely, avoiding contact.*

SIDE ELBOW STRIKE—APPLICATION

Side Elbow Strike (*Empi-uchi*) Application [Figures 1-2]

Fig. 1   Assuming the natural stance, block the attacker's upper attack from the right side.

Fig. 2   Grab the attacking arm with the left hand.

Side Elbow Strike (*Empi-uchi*) Application [Figures 3-4]

Fig. 3   Bring the right arm across the midsection of the body with the palm of the fist facing upward.

Fig. 4   Slide closer to the attacker with the right foot and execute the side elbow strike. Observe that the palm faces downward at the completion of the technique.

BACK ELBOW STRIKE—APPLICATION

Back Elbow Strike (*Empi-uchi*) Application [Figures 1-3]

Fig. 1 Begin in natural stance, and the attacker executes a one-arm choke from behind.

Fig. 2 Extend the left arm straight forward with the fist palm side downward.

Fig. 3 Stepping back with the left foot, simultaneously thrust the striking elbow back as shown, with the palm side upward. This motion follows the path of retracting arm and hand from a front middle-punch.

FRONT ELBOW STRIKE—APPLICATION

Front Elbow Strike (*Empi-uchi*) Application [Figures 1-2]

Fig. 1 An attacker executes an upper lunge punch. Block the attack with the right arm while stepping back with the left foot to assume half-and-half stance.

Fig. 2 Use the left, open hand to press the attacker's arm downward and to the side. Simultaneously pull the right foot back slightly and pivot the body to the right.

Front Elbow Strike (*Empi-uchi*) Application [Figures 3-4]

Fig. 3 Step forward with the foot to the outside of the attacker's right foot to prepare for execution of the front elbow strike.

Fig. 4 Use a right elbow to strike the attacker's right midsection. Depending on the position in relation to the attacker, the elbow strike can be executed to the solar plexus, the ribcage or temple.

DOWNWARD ELBOW STRIKE—APPLICATION

Downward Elbow Strike (*Empi-uchi*) Application [Figures 1-3]

Fig. 1-2 Face the attacker in a ready-to-defend stance. The attacker lunges forward in an attempt to tackle the defender. To stop the attack, press the attacker's head down and forward with an open hand.

Fig. 3 Step back with the right foot and take the attacker down to the floor by pulling the attacker forward. Raise the right arm high with the fist showing its palm side away. Execute the strike to the base of the attacker's skull. The right knee touches the floor with the execution of the technique.

Make sure that the downward elbow strike is executed in such a way that the fist twists, and at the completion of the technique the palm side is toward the face, as shown.

Section 8 – Spear Hand Strike (*Nukite*)

Spear Hand Strike (*Nukite*) [Figures 1-2]

Fig. 1 Block the attacker's right middle punch with a left palm heel block.

Fig. 2 Shift weight onto the left leg and deliver a right spear-hand strike to the attacker's throat.

Two-finger Spear Hand Strike (*Nihon-nukite*) [Figure 3-5]

Fig. 3 The spear-hand strike can be used against the attacker's eye in the form of a two-finger spear hand (*nihon-nukite*). *Nihon-nukite* can also be executed against the attacker's throat (not shown).

Section 9 – Palm Heel Strike (*Teisho-uchi*)

Fig. 1   Block the attacker's right upper punch with the left arm.

Fig. 2   Grab the attacking arm and deliver the palm heel strike to the attacker's chin. The palm heel strike is executed in the same manner as the regular punch.

Fig. 3   The palm heel strike can also be executed against the attacker's jaw.

Palm Heel Strike (*Teisho-uchi*) [Figures 1-3]

Palm Heel Strike (*Teisho-uchi*) [Figures 4-5]

Fig. 3   Following an open hand circular block, the palm heel strike can also be executed a strike to the glabella (space between the eyebrows) or philtrum (space between the nose and the upper lip.)

CHAPTER 15

Kicking and Striking
The Use of Feet and Legs in Self-Defense

Section 1 – Benefits and Mechanics of Kicking and Striking with Feet and Legs

The main advantages of using the legs in self-defense are, of course, their reach and their power. If you have to deal with an attacker that is physically larger than you, it may be necessary to take advantage of your kicking ability. The use of legs and feet can offset an attacker's balance or create an opening for an effective hand technique to end a fight. Legs and feet are also effective finishing weapons.

Balance is critical in any self-defense technique, but especially in foot and leg techniques. The importance of a grounded supporting foot cannot be over emphasized. In the beginning stages of your training, you are bound to feel awkward and unstable as you try to stand on one leg while kicking with the other. The supporting foot should be placed flat on the ground as you kick with the other leg so that you can absorb the impact of your kick without breaking balance. For the maximum effect, it is important to push your hips and stomach toward the target at the moment you execute the technique.

SNAP KICK AND THRUST KICK

There are two methods of delivery in kicking techniques: snapping motion and thrusting motion. The snap kick uses flexibility of the knee and the pull-back of the leg, as if in a whipping motion to deliver the power of the kick. The thrust kick engages the strength of the hips and combines that with the snap motion of the knee to create a powerful impact on the target. The thrust kick is more commonly used in self-defense.

As for the supporting foot, in the case of the snap kick it normally does not move but should be strong and stable. In the case of the thrust kick, the supporting foot may move slightly in order to engage power from the hip fully.

Section 2 – Front Kick (*Mae-geri*)

Front Kick (*Mae-geri*) [Figures 1-3]

Figs. 1-3 Bring the right knee up and extend the right foot forward, make sure that the ankle is fully flexed so that the ball of the kicking foot is directed to the target.

Front Kick (*Mae-geri*) [Figures 4-5]

Figs. 4-5 Fully extend the leg to reach the target, and then pull the foot back following the same path that it went out.

NOTE: One's balance and center of gravity must be centered over a stable supporting foot in order to execute a strong kick.

Front Kick (*Mae-geri*) Application [Figures 6-7]

Figs. 6-7 The front kick can be executed in attacks to the leg (not shown), groin, and midsection depending on the situation.

Front Kick (*Mae-geri*) Application [Figure 8]

Fig. 8 The front kick can also be executed to the face.

NOTE: In an actual self-defense situation, it is highly unlikely that one would use such a high front kick, but it can be good for practice.

Section 3 – Front Kick (*Mae-geri*): Stepping to Front Kick Practice

Figs. 1-8 Start in natural stance. Raise fisted hands while step forward with the left foot to minor front stance and perform a right front kick. Then put the right foot back down to resumes natural stance. Perform the same series with the opposite leg. This sequence should be practice as a continuous fluid motion.

VARIATION (NOT SHOWN)

Start in natural stance with hands up, step forward with the left foot into a ready-to-defend stance and execute a right front kick. Then step the right foot down in front of the left into another ready-to-defend stance and perform a left front kick. Continue to alternate kicking legs.

Front Kick (*Mae-geri*): Stepping to Front Kick Practice

Section 4 – Side Kick (*Yoko-geri*)

Side Kick (*Yoko-geri*) [Figures 1-2]

Figs. 1-2 Bring the knee of the kicking foot up high so the kicking foot is facing the same direction as the supporting foot.

Side Kick (*Yoko-geri*) [Figures 3-4]

Figs. 3-4 Execute a side kick to the lower leg or midsection of an imaginary attacker. The edge of the kicking foot would strike the target with its toes curled up. In the thrust side kick, it travels in the shortest distance possible (straight line to the target).

Side Kick (*Yoko-geri*) Application [Figures 5-7]

Figs. 5-7   Adjust the supporting foot to the correct distance for the kick. This takes practice and experience. Execute the side kick to the attacker's shin, midsection or throat. The supporting foot must be stable for an effective kick. In practice, one must be careful not to make any contact with the partner's body.

Side Kick (*Yoko-geri*) Application [Figures 8-10]

Figs. 8-10   In an actual self-defense situation, a low side kick (thrust) to the attacker's knee, shin or groin area can be effective to offset the attacker's aggression. Here the side thrust kick is used to attacked the vital point behind the knee.

Section 5 – Roundhouse Kick (*Mawashi-geri*)

Roundhouse Kick (*Mawashi-geri*) [Figures 1-3]

Figs. 1-2 Bring the kicking knee and foot high at a 45-degree angle with toes curled up in preparation for the kick.

Fig. 3 Extend the kicking foot out in an arcing motion. The supporting foot turns about 90 degrees in the direction of the kick to accommodate the kicking motion.

Roundhouse Kick (*Mawashi-geri*) [Figures 4-5]

Figs. 4-5 Fully extend the leg to reach the target with the ball of the foot, and then pull the foot back following the same path that it went out.

Roundhouse Kick (*Mawashi-geri*) Application [Figures 6-8]

Figs. 6-8 A roundhouse kick can be effective in a real self-defense situation when executed to the solar plexus, groin or knee.

Roundhouse Kick (*Mawashi-geri*) Application [Figure 9]

Fig. 9   A more advanced application shown here is a kick to the attacker's temple; however, this type of kick is rarely used in a self-defense situation.

Section 6 – Back Kick (*Ushiro-geri*)

Back Kick (*Ushiro-geri*) [Figures 1-3]

Figs. 1-3 Bring the knee up and raise the kicking foot high while looking over the shoulder towards the target. The supporting foot points away from the target.

Back Kick (*Ushiro-geri*) [Figures 4-5]

Figs. 4-5 Extend the leg straight back with the toes of the kicking foot pointed downward as the heel goes out in a straight line. The point of contact is the heel and its target is the solar plexus or chin. Make sure to pull the kicking leg back quickly.

Back Kick (*Ushiro-geri*) Application [Figures 6-7]

Fig. 6 Raise the kicking foot (the left foot in this case looking over the left shoulder to the target). Depending on the angle of the attacker's body, a back kick can target the solar plexus or floating rib (not shown). Consideration of distance to the attacker is important because it is difficult to adjust quickly when the back is to the attacker.

Fig. 7 The kick can also be executed to the throat or face. Strictly observe the no-contact rule in practice.

Back Kick (*Ushiro-geri*) [Figure 8]

Fig. 8 The back kick may also be done from the ground which can provide more strength and stability to the kick.

Section 7 – Stamping Kick (*Fumikomi-geri*)

In stamping kick, the heel or the foot-edge are used in a stamping motion. This kick is most commonly used to strike an attacker at the knee, shin, ankle or foot, as shown in figures 1-4. It is also used to strike to the head or neck after a take down, as shown in figure 5.

Stamping Kick (*Fumikomi-geri*) [Figures 1-5]

Section 8 – Front Knee Kick (*Mae-hiza-geri*)

Knee kick techniques may be performed as strikes straight up and toward the front or moving in a circular motion from the side of the body to the front. These kicking techniques are especially well-suited to situations in which the attacker is close.

Front Knee Kick (*Mae-hiza-geri*) [Figure 1]

Fig. 1   The front knee kick is performed straight up and towards the target. Shown here is a front knee kick to the face but the solar plexus or abdomen are also potential targets.

Section 9 – Roundhouse Knee Kick (*Mawashi-hiza-geri*)

Roundhouse Knee Kick (*Mawashi-hiza-geri*) Application [Figure 1]

Fig. 1   The roundhouse knee moves in an arcing motion from the side of the body to the front similar to the roundhouse kick. As with the front knee kick, the striking areas include the face and midsection.

NOTE: Both the front and roundhouse knee kick are especially well-suited to fighting when one is close to an attacker.

CHAPTER 16

Kata (Form)
The Importance of Prearranged Forms in Self-Defense Training

A well-executed kata has, among other things, a symbolic value: it is a living example of self-control. I choose to put my foot here; I put it exactly here. The same with every movement—every punch, block, and kick is focused precisely. Students will appreciate such things if it is demonstrated. They will see that self-control is an ultimate goal of training. Without self-control, it is very difficult to live in harmony with others or at peace with one's self.

With the addition of an aesthetic component in traditional marital art training, abstract movements in pre-arranged forms (kata) became prevalent. These abstract movements are not meaningless; however, for the most part, they can only be understood with training under an authentic teacher over a long period of time. The process used to understand the hidden meaning behind these martial arts moves is called *bun-kai*, or analysis. *Bun-kai* can have several layers of meaning in application (*oh-yoh*) to real self-defense fighting.

Section 1 – Introduction to Kata

Kata, literally translated as "form," is by definition the prearranged and systematized formal exercise of fighting movements against imaginary opponents. In kata, various block and attacks, together with body-shifting movements, are arranged in a manner according to the number and supposed positions of the opponents. Kata were specifically designed by ancient masters to help students strengthen their fighting skills, because they would best develop the individual's mind, spirit and body.

At the physical level, kata exercises allow students to learn various blocks and attacks arranged in a manner that might be applied to real-life self-defense situations. Various shifting movements are included so that students can successfully keep balance and transfer weight. Furthermore, the type of physical exercise provided by kata practice cannot be found in any other form of exercise, even by continuous sport-sparring. Through systematic repetition, students develop muscle coordination, tone, strength, speed, balance, flexibility and, depending on the energy and effort expanded, improved cardiovascular health. Ultimately, in order to make each movement of a kata alive and meaningful, the student must eventually perform the kata with the appropriate rhythm, balance, speed, power, accuracy and gracefulness that are attained through correct and vigorous training.

At the mental and spiritual levels, kata helps to develop students' concentration, self-discipline, confidence and patience. Although in kata one fights against imaginary opponents, it should be practiced as if one imagines a serious fight and often a deadly combat. It is not a sport-sparring match in which one scores or is scored against. "Fighting" in *kata* is so serious in nature that its performance requires the total fighting spirit and concentration, just as in the case of a true self-defense situation. With continued study, the student will develop increasing levels of proficiency, which will inevitably increase their confidence as well.

In addition, to intensify the students' mental and spiritual development, ancient masters made *kata* difficult to understand by "couching" how some of the underlying techniques could be applied to real-life self-defense situations. Consequently, students need to meditate, or think through each movement and its application to real opponents. The formal analysis of kata that reveals this application is known as *bun-kai*. *Bun-kai* must be learned gradually, as many levels of analysis cannot be fully understood unless the student has reached certain levels of skill. Only through patient and disciplined practice can students discover why each movement in kata had been designed for a particular situation.

Section 2 – *Kihon Kata Sho-dan* (Basic Kata #1): Right and Left (*Migi* and *Hidari*)

Kihon Kata Sho-dan [Figures 1-3]

Figs. 1-3 Start in attention stance with feet together at a 45-degree angle, your back is straight, shoulders relaxed and down with hands at your sides. Bow to show respect prior to doing the kata and return to attention stance.

Kihon Kata Sho-dan [Figures 4-5]

Figs. 4-5 Make fists and cross your arms at your wrists with the right arm on the outside. Step your left foot out as your arms go into position, out towards your sides and slightly in front of your body.

ART AND THEORY OF SELF-DEFENSE | 141

Kihon Kata Sho-dan [Figures 6-7]

Figs. 6-7 Put your left fist, pinky finger side touching your right shoulder. Step your left foot straight forward into a front stance as you do a left downward block.

Kihon Kata Sho-dan [Figures 8-10]

Figs. 8-9 Step forward with your right foot, using the crescent step (see Ch. 11, Section 3), into a front stance. Execute a right middle punch and ki-ai (see Ch. 5, Section 1) as you finish the stance.

Fig. 10 Raise your right arm into an upper block position with your hand open and palm facing outward.

***Kihon Kata Sho-dan* [Figures 11-13]**

Figs. 11-13 Bring your left foot forward and in towards the right foot, using the crescent step to go into a left front stance as you start your upper block. Move your left arm across and up in front of the middle of your body as you pull your right arm towards your right hip. Simultaneously finish the left upper block and left front stance.

***Kihon Kata Sho-dan* [Figures 14-16]**

Figs. 14-15 Move your right foot forward, using the crescent step (see Chapter 11, Section 3), into a front stance. Execute a right upper punch and *ki-ai* with the punch, as your right foot lands in a right front stance.

Fig. 16 Cross your arms at your wrists with the right arm on the outside.

Kihon Kata Sho-dan [Figures 17-19]

Figs. 17-19 Keep your arms crossed and move your left foot straight forward. Place your left foot under your left shoulder so you are in a natural stance with your arms crossed. Straighten your arms so they are down towards your sides and slightly in front of your body.

OPTIONAL CONCLUSION: Right Side Practice Only of *Kihon Kata Sho-Dan*

NOTE: At this point, in practice of **Kihon Kata Shodan**, the instructor may conclude by bringing the left foot to the right in attention stance and bow.

Otherwise, the practice may continue to practice the left side of the kata (bow would be omitted) and move forward to the next images, which show right downward block.

Kihon Kata Sho-dan **[Figures 20-21]**

Figs. 20-21 Start in natural stance with arms down. Bring your right fist, pinky finger side to your left shoulder.

Kihon Kata Sho-dan **[Figures 22-23]**

Figs. 22-23 Step right foot straight forward into a front stance as your right fist moves down your extended left arm. As you finish stepping into a right front stance, complete a right downward block.

Kihon Kata Sho-dan **[Figures 24-25]**

Figs. 24-25   Bring your left foot forward into a front stance using the crescent step. Execute a left middle punch with a *ki-ai* as you execute the punch and your left front stance.

Kihon Kata Sho-dan **[Figures 26-28]**

Figs. 26-28   Raise your left arm into an upper block position and open your left hand so the palm side is facing outward. Bring your right foot forward, using the crescent step, and begin to move your right arm for a right upper block. Execute your right upper block as you step your right foot in a right front stance.

Kihon Kata Sho-dan **[Figures 29-30]**

Figs. 29-30 Bring your left foot forward into a front stance using the crescent step and execute a left upper punch with a *ki-ai* as you complete your left front stance.

Kihon Kata Sho-dan **[Figures 31-32]**

Figs. 31-32 Cross your arms at your wrists with the right arm on the outside. Keep your arms crossed and step your right foot forward into a natural stance.

Kihon Kata Sho-dan [Figures 33-34]

Figs. 33-34 Straighten your arms so they are down towards your sides and slightly in front of your body in a natural stance.

Kihon Kata Sho-dan [Figures 35-37]

Figs. 35-37 Go back to attention stance, bow, and finish in attention stance.

Section 3 – *Kihon Kata Ni-dan* (not shown)

Kihon Kata Nidan is identical to ***Kihon Kata Sho-dan*** except that a front kick is inserted after each downward block and before each lunge punch. For example, after Figure 7 and before Figure 8, shown above in ***Kihon Kata Sho-dan***, the fists would be raised in ready-to-defend position (below), and a right front kick would be executed. The right foot (kicking foot) would then land in right foot forward front stance, as a right lunge punch is executed with *ki-ai*.

Preparatory Posture and the Start of Front Kick in *Kihon Kata Ni-dan*

Section 4– *Kihon Kata San-dan and Yon-dan*: Line of Performance (*Enbusen*)

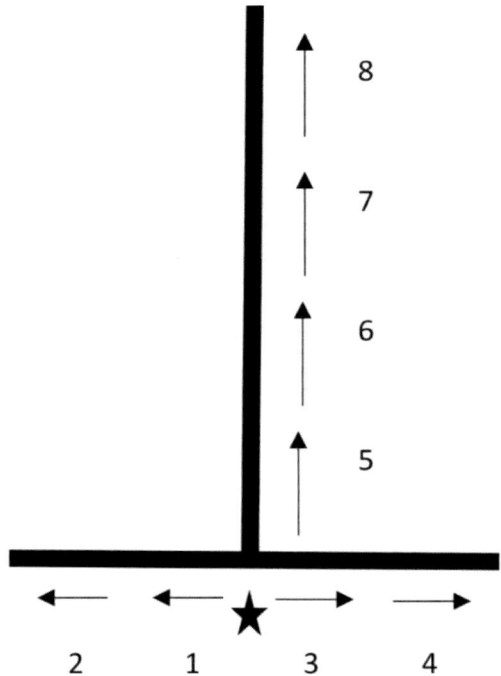

1. Downward Block (Left)
2. Right Middle Lunge Punch
3. Downward Block (Right)
4. Left Middle Lunge Punch
5. Downward Block (Left)
6. Right Middle Lunge Punch
7. Left Middle Lunge Punch
8. Right Middle Lunge Punch

Section 5 – *Kihon Kata San-dan*

Kihon Kata San-dan [Figures 1-3]

Figs. 1-3 Start in attention stance with feet together at a 45-degree angle, your back is straight, shoulders relaxed and down, with hands at your sides, and then bow. Return to attention stance (not shown), make fists and cross your arms at your wrists with the right arm on the outside.

Kihon Kata San-dan [Figures 4-6]

Fig. 4 Slide the left foot out to the left side as your arms go into position—towards the sides and slightly in front of the body.

Figs. 5-6 Place the left fist, pinky finger side at the right shoulder. Step left foot out to the left side into a left front stance as execute a left down block.

ART AND THEORY OF SELF-DEFENSE | 151

Kihon Kata San-dan **[Figures 7-9]**

Fig. 7 Step into a right front stance and execute a right middle punch.

Figs. 8-9 Bring the right fist to the left shoulder, pinky side touching the shoulder as you move the right foot behind you in a diagonal direction. Pivot clockwise towards the right and execute right downward block to the right.

Kihon Kata San-dan **[Figures 10-11]**

Fig. 10 Step into a left front stance and execute a left middle punch.

Fig. 11 Bring the left fist to your right shoulder and the left foot back to your right foot and turn your body towards the front.

Kihon Kata San-dan **[Figures 12-14]**

Figs. 12-14 Move the left foot out into a left front stance facing back towards the front as you execute a left downward block. Step into a right front stance and execute a right middle punch. Then, step into a left front stance and execute a left middle punch.

Kihon Kata San-dan **[Figures 15-16]**

Figs. 15-16 Step using the crescent step with the right foot into a right front stance and execute a right middle punch with a *ki-ai*.

Kihon Kata San-dan [Figures 17-18]

Figs. 17-18 Cross your arms at your wrists with the right arm on the outside and step your left foot forward into a natural stance as you straighten your arms to ready position.

Kihon Kata San-dan [Figures 19-21]

Figs. 19-21 Pull your left foot in to attention stance with your arms at your sides, bow, and finish in attention stance.

Section 6 – *Kihon Kata Yon-dan*

Kihon Kata Yon-dan (complete kata not shown) is identical to *Kihon Kata San-dan* except for two differences. One, the blocks which are executed to the West and to the East are **middle inside/outside blocks** (Figure 1 below and see Chapter 13: Section 3) instead of downward blocks (as shown). Two, the series of three punches to the North are **upper punches** instead of middle punches (Figure 2 below).

Kihon Kata Yon-dan: Execution of Middle Inside Outside Block to the West [Figure 1]

Kihon Kata Yon-dan: Execution of the First of Three Upper Punches to the North [Figure 2]

CHAPTER 17

Blocker Training Methods

Executing an effective block or self-defense strike requires the coordination of the mind, body and breath. The use of blockers and focus targets is beneficial in self-defense training on several levels. First, it allows one's mind and body to experience receiving and delivering a punch, a strike or a kick without injury. At the beginning, it can be very jarring or frightening for a person to feel being struck by an object. It's important to overcome this tendency. In self-defense, the mind must remain steady and composed.

Second, incorporating these devices in a training program will advance a student's technical skill. Blocker practice drills improve proper formation and timing of blocks, as well as visual awareness. Focus target drills develop proper execution of punches, strikes and kicks. When a fist or foot contacts a target, deficiencies in technique become apparent, such as a slight bend in the wrist during a punch. Target training also improves one's ability to judge the proper distancing, called *ma-ai*, which allows for the correct positioning of the body and extension of the joints and limbs to make solid contact with the target.

Third, these drills require mutual cooperation and trust, which contribute to an important lesson in civility, such as respecting each other's individuality and contributing to another's well-being and learning.

Section 1 – Blocker Technique 1: "Wall of Confidence"

Blocker Technique 1: "Wall of Confidence" [Figures 1-3]

Figs. 1-2 Gently walk in place four times, starting with the either foot to relax the body and return to natural stance with fists up in ready position.

Fig. 3 In natural stance, execute a left upper block.

Blocker Technique 1: "Wall of Confidence" [Figures 4-6]

Figs. 4-6 In natural stance, execute right upper block, left down block to the left side and right down block to the right side in response to sideways attacks.

Section 2 – Blocker Technique 2: Upper Block and Front Kick

Blocker Technique 2: Upper Block and Front Kick [Figures 1-3]

Figs. 1-3 In natural stance execute left upper block. The execution of the block is timed to receive strike from the blocker at the moment of the impact above and in front of the forehead.

Blocker Technique 2: Upper Block and Front Kick [Figures 4-6]

Figs. 4-6 In natural stance raise the fists in "ready-to-defend" position and execute a left front snap kick, first raising the left knee and then kicking.

Blocker Technique 2: Upper Block and Front Kick [Figures 7-9]

Fig. 7 It is important to fully pull back the kicking foot with the knee up.

Figs. 8-9 Return to natural stance. Immediately prepare for a right upper block. Execute right upper block.

Blocker Technique 2: Upper Block and Front Kick [Figures 10-12]

Figs. 10-12 In natural stance raise the fists in "ready to defend" forward and execute a right front snap kick with the hands up. Return to natural stance.

Section 3 – Blocker Technique 3: Push to Back

Blocker Technique 3: Push to Back [Figures 1-3]

Figs. 1-3   Push from blocker comes to the back. Defender turns clockwise and stepping forward with the right foot for balance and then executes a left upper block in response to the up and down strike to the head.

Blocker Technique 3: Push to Back [Figures 4-6]

Figs. 4-6   The defender then executes left front kick. The knee is lifted in preparation for the kick. Then, at execution of the kick, the leg is straight and the blocker has been thrown upward by the kick. Finish with the hands up with the left foot forward in "ready-to-defend" posture.

NOTE: Blocker Technique: "Push to Back" can also be practiced on the opposite side, in which the defender would turn clockwise at the beginning. The left foot would come forward for balance. A right upper block and front kick would follow, ending in right foot forward "ready to defend" posture.

ART AND THEORY OF SELF-DEFENSE | 161

Section 4 – Blocker Technique 4: Horizontal Strike to Head with Duck and Roundhouse Kick

Blocker Technique 4: Horizontal Strike to Head with Duck and Roundhouse Kick [Figures 1-3]

Begin in natural stance with fists up in ready position, and then gently walk in place four times, starting with the right foot. (Not shown)

Fig. 1 Attacker swings the blocker at head level like a baseball bat.

Figs. 2-3 From natural stance the defender ducks down, keeping the hips higher than the knees, fingertips touch the floor and comes back up and to execute a left roundhouse kick with hands up.

Blocker Technique 4: Horizontal Strike to Head with Duck and Roundhouse Kick [Figures 4-6]

Figs. 4-6 The attacker swings again and defender ducks down keeping the hips higher than the knees. The fingertips touch the floor and comes back up and to execute a right roundhouse kick with hands up. When pulling back from a roundhouse kick, it is important to keep the knee high and supporting foot in position until the foot is fully retracted.

CHAPTER 18

Ukemi (Falling Method)

As a part of self-defense knowledge, it is essential to learn the basic falling methods. Falling (*ukemi*) can be a highly refined art in itself, but for the purposes of basic self-defense we concentrate on four primarily falling techniques: back fall, side fall, front fall and front roll to side fall.

The most important aspect of *ukemi* is protecting the head when one lands on the ground. To accomplish this, tuck the chin tightly to the chest and have the feeling of making the body small, like a ball. The arms should strike the ground at the moment the body hits the ground, bearing the weight of the fall. In side falling, receive the whole impact of falling with either arm. In front or back falling, naturally use the two arms, as shown in the following illustrations.

Not only does proficiency in *ukemi* offer a highly useful skill in self-protection, it also directly correlates to the development of one's confidence in handling unexpected loss of balance.

Section 1 – *Ukemi* from Floor: Back Fall from Seated Position and Squat Position

BACK FALL FROM SEATED POSITION

Back Fall from Floor from Seated Position [Figures 1-4]

Fig. 1   From the sitting position, cross the arms in front of the chest with palms facing down.

Fig. 2   To begin the back fall, raise the crossed arms high in front of the forehead, keeping the chin tucked in to the chest.

Fig. 3   To complete the back fall, keep the head up with the chin tightly tucked to the chest. The arms are kept straight and strike the floor about 45 degrees from the sides of the body. The hands slap hard on the floor at the moment of impact. It is important to absorb the shock of falling back by hitting the ground strongly with open hands and arms.

Fig. 4   Do not allow the head to hit the floor. Relax the legs by bending the knees.

BACK FALL FROM FULL SQUAT POSITION

Back Fall from Floor from Full Squat Position [Figures 1-3]

Figs. 1-2   Begin in the standing position. Then take a full squat and cross the arms in front of the chest with palms facing down.

Fig. 3   To begin the back fall, raise the crossed arms high in front of the forehead, keeping the chin tucked in to the chest.

Back Fall from Floor from Full Squat Position [Figures 4-5]

Fig. 3   To complete the back fall, keep the head up with the chin tightly tucked to the chest. The arms are kept straight and strike the floor about 45 degrees from the sides of the body. The hands slap hard on the floor at the moment of impact. It is important to absorb the shock of falling back by hitting the ground strongly with open hands and arms.

Fig. 4   Do not allow the head to hit the floor. Relax the legs by bending the knees.

Section 2 – *Ukemi* from Floor: Side Fall

Side Falls from Floor – Right Side: [Figures 1-2]

Fig. 1   From the sitting position with both legs extended, bring the left arm high with its palm side facing away from the side of the head.

Fig. 2   To execute the side fall, hit the mat with the open hand and whole arm. Make sure the weight of the fall is sustained by the left arm as much as possible with the sensation of making the body small. Bend the knees and keep the head up and away from the floor with the chin tucked in.

NOTE: Generally, the side fall is practiced from the left side first, and then to the right. Right side (shown). Important aspects of side falling practice are:

- To keep the head away from the ground
- To keep the striking arm straight and 45 degrees from the body
- To sustain as much of the weight of the fall as possible with the striking arm
- To keep the legs relaxed by bending the knees slightly and NEVER cross the legs.

Section 3 – *Ukemi* from the Floor: Front Fall

Front Fall: Side View and Front View [Figures 1-2]

Fig. 1   Start in the kneeling position with the hands in front of the face with palms facing forward (away from the head).

Fig. 2   To execute the front fall, land on the forearms and turn the head to the left to protect the face. At the moment when the forearms and hands strike the floor, lift the knees and keep the hips upward in a slight pike position.

NOTE: To become comfortable with falling toward the face during the first few times of practicing front fall, it may be useful to land on the forearms and turn the head to the side to protect the face, while keeping the knees on the ground.

Section 4 – *Ukemi* from Standing Position: Front Roll to Side Fall

Ukemi: **Front Roll to Side Fall [Figures 1-2]**

Fig. 1   From the natural stance, take one step forward with your right foot.

Fig. 2   Place your left hand at the point directly below your left shoulder and in front of your left foot. Bring your right knife hand inside your left hand with its outer edge touching the mat.

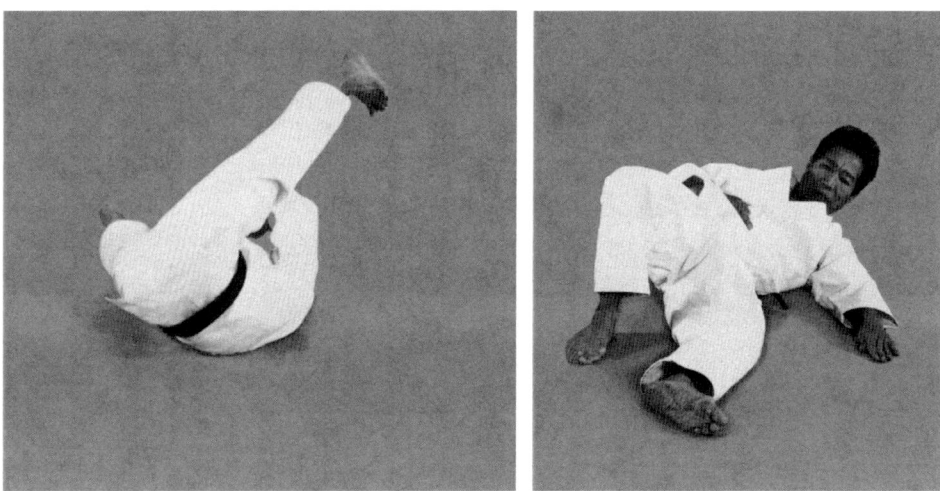

Ukemi: **Front Roll to Side Fall [Figures 3-4]**

Fig. 3   As you start your roll, maintain the sensation of going over your right arm's outer line to your right shoulder, as if your arms form an imaginary wheel. Do not touch your head to the floor..

Fig. 4   As you complete the roll, execute the left arm side fall. Again, keep your head up and chin tucked in toward the chest. To practice the opposite side, start with the left foot forward and bring your left knife hand inside your right hand with its outer edge touching the mat. Take the final fall with the right arm.

NOTE: The front roll can also be finished by using the momentum from the roll to continue into a full standing position, ending in the ready-to-defend posture.

CHAPTER 19

Theory of Situational Self-defense

Section 1 – The Grammar of Self-Defense

In reality, there are an infinite number of potential self-defense situations, and no matter how many self-defense techniques one learns, they can never cover all the scenarios that can occur in life. While we cannot anticipate the details of every potential self-defense situation, we can prepare for the innumerable threats by practicing prearranged techniques, which serve to teach the grammar of self- defense. Just as one learns to communicate by applying grammatical rules to the units of language, such as words, clauses, and phrases, one practices rules of self-defense as they apply to the many elements of self-defense techniques.

Fundamental elements of self-defense techniques are:

1. Stance (*Tachikata*)
2. Block (*Ukekata*)
3. Counterattack—Punch (*Tsuki*), Strike (*Atemi*), Kick (*Keri*)
4. *Ki-ai* (Focused shout to join mind body and breath)
5. Posture (*Kamae*)
6. Power and focus (*Kime*)
7. Creating correct distance (*Ma-ai*)
8. *Zan-shin* (Calm, alert mind in reserve)

NOTE: Four of the above fundamental elements of self-defense technique (stance, block, counterattacks and *ki-ai*) are discussed in earlier chapters. The remaining fundamental elements are discussed in this chapter.

When these elements of self-defense are practiced with prescribed body-shifting motions in prearranged forms, known as *kata*, one will grow increasingly adept at adjusting the mind and body to handle any potentially life-threatening encounter from any direction. Some katas are practiced alone, without partners, and others, known as *goshin no kata*, are practiced by two or more partners, to simulate real self-defense situations.

As with learning any language or art, in self-defense, it is critical to establish a firm grasp of the fundamental elements. With diligent technical practice, following the rules of pre-arranged form, so as not to develop faulty technique; one's ability in self-defense will grow in strength and reliability. Self-defense theory comes alive when practiced with a focused mental attitude, as if engaged in a real self-defense situation.

Section 2 – *Kamae* (Posture)

Generally speaking, the most effective posture in self-defense is upright and perpendicular to the ground. Posture (*kamae*) is considered a basic element in self-defense, because balance is directly affected by how the spine rests on the pelvis. With that in mind, one can see how posture will affect stance, which in turn fosters or inhibits one's ability to hold the ground firmly or to move freely with agility.

Section 3 – *Kime*: Decisive, focused physical and mental power in execution of technique

Kime is the correct and complete use of physiology to execute a technique which is synchronized with correct, complete and decisive mental focus. For example, when delivering a self-defense punch the stance and posture must be correct, with the toes biting the ground, balance and the timing of body rotation must be aligned and coordinated to transmit the power of the legs, hips, and torso to the punching arm and fist. Further, the mind and breath join with the physical techniques in such a way that one's focus is unified—this is often expressed with *ki-ai* and eye focus (*chaku gan*).

The practice of *kime* in self-defense training offers an important bridge for the body and mind to shift from the safety of a training hall to the reality of a life-and-death battle.

Section 4 – *Ma-ai*: Correct distance

Establishing *ma-ai* is creating the correct distance for the execution of a technique, in space and time, to achieve that technique's maximum potential. *Ma-ai* is subjective, in that, the combination of each person's size, skill and speed vary, and therefore each person's *ma-ai*, optimal striking distance and ability to establish that distance, varies.

If one is too far from one's opponent to execute a punch or elbow strike, it will be ineffective no matter how well one may be able to do it. In this case, a kick may be a better defensive technique, but if one has a weak kicking ability, it may be better to find a method to close the distance and execute a knee kick or non-twisting punch.

While *ma-ai* in the example above may seem rather simple, keep in mind that often *ma-ai* constantly shifts. In a real self-defense situation, one's opponent may be moving constantly, rather than remaining still. Establishing one's *ma-ai* requires highly developed awareness, combined with the skill to adapt physical techniques quickly to dominate the opponent.

It's worth noting, *ma-ai* primarily refers to perceiving the requirements of physical distancing between opponents, it also requires the ability to accurately grasp the opponent's mental state, which can reveal an opening for closing physical distance.

Section 5 – *Zan-shin*: The mind that remains to be alert

Literally translated as "remaining mind" or "mind in reserve", *zan-shin* is the state of mind that is alert and ready in calmness to respond not only while techniques are executed, but also after the opponent has been defeated. One must keep balance after the execution of technique(s), which means being ready for any further action if required.

Zan-shin refers to holding onto the mental domination over the opponent after victory has been attained. In pre-arranged self-defense practice, *zan-shin* is expressed with the hands-down and eyes focused on the attacker. In *zan-shin* following combat, physical action is replaced with inner strength and calm by remaining mentally with the fallen opponent to ensure that peace has been restored and will prevail.

Beyond self-defense training, the mental state of *zan-shin* can be carried into daily life, by developing heightened awareness and focus. This awareness can be applied to physical surroundings, to oneself, to others and to undertaking everyday tasks in life at home, work or school. In *zan-shin*, one's inner strength shines in calmness.

Section 6 – The Unwritten Self-Defense Rule: "Get Away, Run Away, Right Away"

Primarily, self-defense training concentrates on the practice of defensive and counter-offensive techniques in pre-arranged forms or drills, combined with breathing and mental-focusing exercises. While this method is centuries old and is sound in preparing one for real self-defense situations, what often goes unsaid and unpracticed is training the mind to make the first choice to leave the dangerous situation before any encounter occurs.

Finding or creating this preemptive window of escape is always the best choice. If this is not a possibility, and self-defense situation requires an escape for a grab or strike, it is always best to flee as quickly as possible, without any further engagement. However, if one's escape from the hold does not result in an opportunity to get away from the danger, one will then need to use a counterattack to sufficiently stop the aggressor(s).

> *Self-defense theory comes alive when practiced with a focused mental attitude, as if one is engaged in a real self-defense situation.*

ABOUT HOW TO PRACTICE SELF-DEFENSE TECHNIQUES

The techniques described in the next several chapters are useful in basic one-to-one self-defense situations, in which no weapons are involved. One might view these techniques as being applicable to situations in which an acquaintance or a stranger suddenly becomes forceful and attacks you in a social situation, such as on a date, in public or at a large gathering. Often the use of a simple, firm technique applied skillfully will adequately discourage further escalation of aggression and open an opportunity for escape.

It is important to follow each technique step by step. As mentioned earlier, pre-arranged self-defense techniques are the grammar for defending oneself from different attack scenarios. *Don't be deceived by the apparent simplicity of these techniques. Though a few practice sessions might give one the impression of having acquired sufficient familiarity, this is certainly not the case. Only repetitive, systematic practice will result in executing these techniques correctly and instinctively in a real situation— during practice, be focused, patient, and remember*

CHAPTER 20

Basic Self-Defense Techniques

Section 1 – Cross-Single Wrist Grab with Anchor

Cross-Single Wrist Grab with Anchor [Figures 1-2]

Fig. 1   Attacker's right hand grabs the defender's right wrist.

Fig. 2   Defender steps in with the right foot and grabs (anchor) the attacker's right wrist. The defender's anchoring grip isolates the attacker's thumb from its corresponding fingers in such a way that the defender can exploit the inherent weakness of the thumb.

 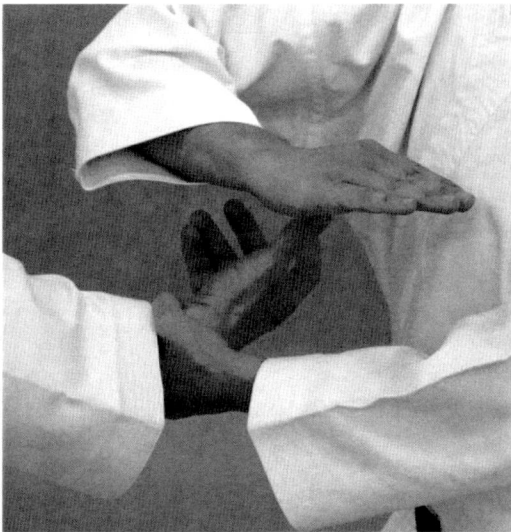

Cross-Single Wrist Grab with Anchor [Figures 3-4]

Figs. 3-4 The defender twists his/her forearm and wrist against the attacker's right thumb, ending in the hand position shown. By applying relatively little force against the thumb, the technique works effectively.

NOTE: This can be practiced on the opposite side. It is important that the defender always steps in with foot that is on the same side as wrist that is being grabbed. This gives balance and leverage.

Section 2 – Cross-Single Wrist Grab without Anchor

Cross-Single Wrist Grab without Anchor [Figures 1-2]

Fig. 1 Attacker's right hand grabs the right wrist.

Fig. 2 Defender steps in firmly with forward force with the right foot while simultaneously twisting his/her forearm and wrist against the attacker's right thumb. The palm side of hand is facing the ground.

Cross-Single Wrist Grab without Anchor [Figures 3-4]

Fig. 3 If needed, the defender can thrust the right elbow into the attacker's solar plexus as a counterattack after the escape from the wrist grab.

Fig. 4 Opposite view of strike to the attacker's solar plexus.

NOTE: Caution should be taken when performing this technique with elbow strike counterattack.

Section 3 – Straight-Single Wrist Grab without Anchor

Straight-Single Wrist Grab without Anchor [Figures 1-3]

Fig. 1 Stepping in, the attacker's right hand grabs the defender's left wrist.

Figs. 2-3 The defender steps in with the left foot, while simultaneously thrusting the left elbow upward toward the attacker's chin. Again, this escape for the wrist hold exploits the weakness of the attacker's thumb.

NOTE: Caution should be taken when performing this technique with elbow strike counterattack.

Section 4 – Double-Wrist Grab Lower

Double-Wrist Grab Lower [Figures 1-3]

Fig. 1 Attacker grabs both of the defender's wrists simultaneously.

Figs. 2-3 The defender steps in, makes fists, and twists his/her hands upward against the attacker's thumbs in such a way that the fists have their palm sides up, at first, and continue upward in such a way that the palms face downward toward the shoulders and the elbows point towards the attacker's chest.

Section 5 – Double-Wrist Grab Higher

Double-Wrist Grab Higher [Figures 1-3]

Fig. 1   The defender's hands are held upward on either side of the head with elbows bent. The attacker grabs each wrist.

Figs. 2-3   The defender steps back with the left foot and "takes-off" against the attacker's thumbs by swinging his/her arms down and out, similar to the "safe" gesture of a baseball umpire.

ONE COUNTERATTACK FOR DOUBLE-WRIST GRAB HIGHER

Counterattack Option #1 for Double-Wrist Grab Higher [Figures 1-3]

Figs. 1-3   The defender slides in with right foot to execute a right upper elbow strike to attacker's chin.

Section 6 – Single Wrist Grab by Two Hands

Single Wrist Grab by Two Hands [Figures 1-3]

Fig. 1   Attacker grabs the right arm with two hands.

Figs. 2-3   The defender steps in with the right foot and clasps hands together without interlocking fingers by bringing the left hand between the attacker's forearms.

Single Wrist Grab by Two Hands [Figures 4-6]

Figs. 4-6   The defender adjusts left foot behind right foot placing the heels in line. Then, the defender pulls the hands straight back to the sternum (breastbone), exploiting the weakness of the thumbs. Keep the shoulders square to the front when the hands pull back, while shifting the weight to the back leg.

NOTE: As with many single-sided techniques, it is important to practice this technique on both the right and left sides.

ONE COUNTERATTACK FOR SINGLE-WRIST GRAB BY TWO HANDS

Counterattack for Single-Wrist Grab by Two Hands [Figures 1-2]

Figs. 1-2   Slide in with the right foot and thrust the knuckles of double-hand flat fist to the attacker's philtrum.

Section 7 – Two-Hand Choke or Grab from the Front to Breaking Balance at Knee (*Hiza-kuzushi*)

Two-Hand Choke or Grab from the Front to Breaking Balance at Knee [Figures 1-2]

Figs. 1-2 The attacker emulates a choking or grabbing motion by placing both hands on the front of the defender's shoulders. The defender clasps his/her hands together without interlocking fingers (making a 90-degree wedge with the forearms). The defender adjusts his/her feet slightly wider into sumo, or stamping, stance and squats down, keeping the back straight and hips above the knees.

Two-Hand Choke or Grab from the Front to Breaking Balance at Knee [Figures 3-4]

Fig. 3 The defender pushes his/her arms straight up using the strength of the legs without unclasping the hands or changing the angle of the wedge of the arms to make contact with the attacker's forearms to release the hold.

Fig. 4 The defender moves his/her right foot forward and executes a right front elbow strike to the attacker's midsection with the hands still clasped together.

Two-Hand Choke or Grab from the Front to Breaking Balance at Knee [Figures 5-6]

Fig. 5   The defender then drops down onto the right knee, grabs the attacker's right ankle with the left hand, and places his/her right forearm on the inside of the attacker's knee.

Fig. 6   The defender then pushes his/her right forearm forward and pulls the left hand backward to take the attacker down. It is critical that the right forearm be properly placed for this technique to work. The attacker's knee is very weak when pushed from the inside. If the forearm is correctly placed, the take-down does not require brute force.

Section 8 – Two-Hand Choke or Grab from Behind – Escape Only

Two-Hand Choke or Grab from Behind [Figures 1-3]

Figs. 1-3 Attacker emulates choking or grabbing motion by placing hand on the back of the defender's shoulders. Defender adjusts the right foot in towards the left foot.

Two-Hand Choke or Grab from Behind [Figures 4-5]

Figs. 4-5 The defender then adjusts left foot out so the feet are in a straight line with palms inwards and turns his/her palms away while spinning clockwise, keeping bodyweight on the left foot with a bent left knee to stay back from attacker. "*Get away, run away, right away!*"

Section 9 – Two-Hand Choke or Grab from Behind to Outer Major Sweep

One possible counterattack to follow the escape from a two-hand choke or grab from behind is to use the outer major sweep.

Counterattack of Outer Major Sweep Two-Hand Choke or Grab from Behind [Figures 1-3]

Figs. 1-2 Having completed the escape shown in Section 8 above, the defender then grabs the attacker's right arm at the shoulder with the left hand.

Fig. 3 The defender places his/her left foot forward outside of the attacker's right foot and at the same time strikes the attacker's jaw with the fleshy part of the outer side of the right palm.

Counterattack of Outer Major Sweep Two-Hand Choke or Grab from Behind [Figures 4-5]

Figs. 4-5 The defender performs the outer major sweep by bringing his/her right foot past the attacker's right foot and then sweeping in an arcing motion with the right calf making contact at the attacker's calf.

Counterattack of Outer Major Sweep Two-Hand Choke or Grab from Behind [Figures 6-7]

Figs. 6-7 While sweeping the leg, the defender pushes his/her right hand against the attacker's jaw and continues to holds to the attacker's right arm with the left hand during the sweep and after the attacker has fallen.

NOTE: Before practicing this technique, it is important to have practiced *ukemi* (falling method).

ART AND THEORY OF SELF-DEFENSE | 185

Section 10 – One-Arm (Bare-Arm) Choke from Behind

One-Arm (Bare-Arm) Choke from Behind [Figures 1-2]

Figs. 1-2 The attacker comes from behind and chokes with the right arm. Immediately the defender tucks his/her chin to the chest.

One-Arm (Bare-Arm) Choke from Behind [Figures 3-4]

Figs. 3-4 The defender uses the right hand to grab the fist and the left hand to grab just above the elbow of the attacker's right arm. Then, the defender adjusts the left foot inward and the right foot forward *to place the feet in a straight line.*

One-Arm (Bare-Arm) Choke from Behind [Figures 5-7]

Figs. 5-7   The defender escapes from the hold by sinking down (bending the knees) while spinning counter-clockwise, pushing and twisting his/her head towards attacker's armpit.

One-Arm (Bare-Arm) Choke from Behind [Figure 8]

Fig. 8   The defender then brings the attacker's right hand on top of their middle back while still holding onto the elbow area with the right hand. From this position the arm can be locked on the back to the attacker, allowing for counterattacks or submission of the attacker on the ground.

CONTINUATION TO COUNTERATTACK OF KNEE KICK FOR ONE-ARM CHOKE FROM BEHIND

Counterattack for One-Arm (Bare-Arm) Choke from Behind [Figures 1-2]

Figs. 1-2   The defender executes a right front knee kick to the solar plexus (as shown) or roundhouse kick to the solar plexus depending on the body position of the attacker.

Section 11 – Bear Hug from Behind

Bear Hug from Behind [Figures 1-3]

Figs. 1-3 The attacker holds the defender from behind with a bear hug. The defender relaxes the body and arms. Then clasps the hands in front of solar plexus and pushes them downward with both elbows tightly rubbing the lower ribs.

Bear Hug from Behind [Figures 4-6]

Figs. 4-6 The defender adjusts the left foot inward, then steps the right foot forward while pushing the head against the attacker's chest and dropping down on one knee all the while twisting the upper body counterclockwise and grabbing the attacker's arms. Once freed from the attacker's hold, immediately recover balance to get away from the attacker or to execute a counterattack

CHAPTER 21

Throws ~ Sweeps ~ Submissions

Unlike striking techniques with the hands, arms, feet and legs, which are known as *goh-no waza* or hard techniques, another important set of techniques in self-defense is known as *ju-no waza* or soft techniques. Soft techniques include throws, sweeps and submissions and are mainly derived from the ancient art of *jujitsu* and modern-day judo.

All of these takedown techniques should be practiced only by those who are familiar with proper falling techniques, known as *ukemi*, (see Chapter 18: *Ukemi*).

Section 1 – Basic Wrist Throw (*Kote-nage*)

Basic Wrist Throw (*Kote-nage*) [Figures 1-2]

Figs. 1-2 The attacker's right hand grabs the defender's right wrist. (Practice this technique and all other techniques on the right and left side). The defender raises his/her right arm turning the palm away and grabs the attacker's right wrist with the left hand as shown.

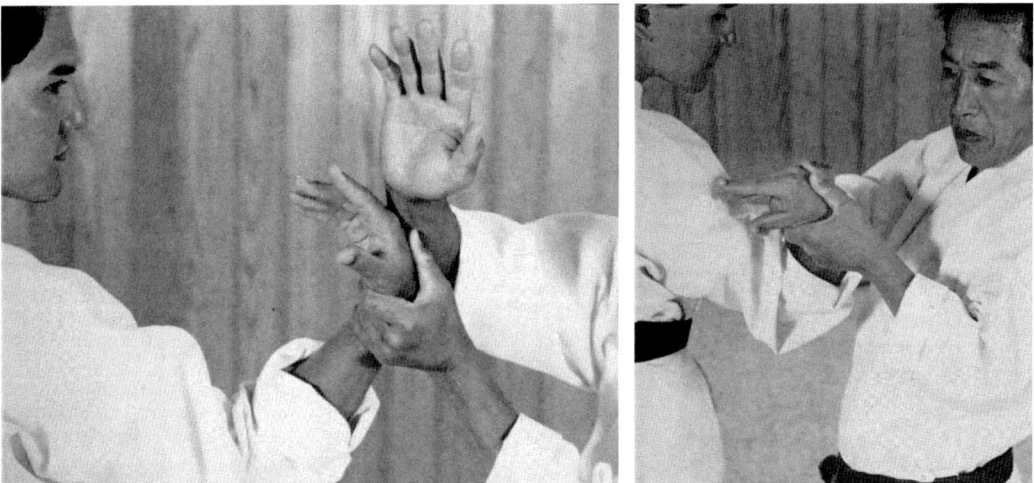

Basic Wrist Throw (*Kote-nage*) [Figures 3-4]

Fig. 3   Upon releasing the grip of the attacker, the defender continues to press on the back of the attacker's hand.

Fig. 4   The defender then uses both hands to grab the attacker's hand and wrist, twisting counter-clockwise and downward, placing pressure on the wrist and elbow joints of the attacker.

Basic Wrist Throw (*Kote-nage*) [Figures 5-6]

Figs. 5-6   The defender steps in with his/her left foot and throws the attacker backward gently by applying extra pressure on the attacker's wrist. When performing this technique on the other side, the defender would step in with his/her right foot.

NOTE: Make sure the attacker knows how to fall properly before executing the throw. It goes without saying that all self-defense techniques need to be practiced with respect and safety. In particular, this technique places torqueing pressure on the joints, and needs to be practiced slowly and gently to avoid injury.

Section 2 – Shoulder Throw (*Seoi-nage*) from One-Arm Choke from Behind

Shoulder Throw (*Seoi-nage*) from One-Arm Choke from Behind [Figures 1-2]

Figs. 1-2 The attacker holds the defender from behind with a one arm choke. The defender tucks the chin down to protect the throat and grabs the attacker's right arm with the right hand.

Shoulder Throw (*Seoi-nage*) from One-Arm Choke from Behind [Figures 3-4]

Figs. 3-4 The defender moves the right foot inside the attacker's right foot. Then the defender moves the left foot back closer to the attacker's left foot with the knees bent. To execute an effect shoulder throw the defender synchronizes three factors: the springing motion with the knees, the strength of the hips and the pulling motion of the right arm (down and across the body).

Shoulder Throw (*Seoi-nage*) from One-Arm Choke from Behind [Figure 5-6]

Figs. 5-6   During the execution of the throw, the defender's right hand keeps holding the attacker's right arm. An optional kick to the head can be used as a finishing technique.

Section 3 – Hip Throw (*Koshi-nage*)

Hip Throw (*Koshi-nage*) [Figures 1-2]

Figs. 1-2   The defender blocks the attacker's left upper reverse punch with the right arm. The defender adjusts the left foot inside closer to the attacker's left foot while holding the attacker's left arm with the right hand.

Hip Throw (Koshi-nage) [Figures 3-4]

Figs. 3-4   The defender wraps the left arm around the attacker's lower back while adjusting the right foot inside the attacker's right foot. The defender synchronizes the : the springing motion of the knees and hips, while using the arms to throw the attacker over the lower back.

Hip Throw (*Koshi-nage*) [Figure 5]

Fig. 5   The defender keeps holding the attacker's left arm in order to execute a punch to the head as an optional finishing technique. The hip throw can be practiced in a slow motion at the beginning.

Section 4 – Scissor Throw (*Hasami Nage*)

Scissor Throw (*Hasami -nage*) [Figures 1-2]

Fig. 1   The defender executes a left upper block against the attacker's upper punch while adjusting the right foot back into half-and-half stance.

Fig. 2   The defender adjusts the right foot slightly closer to attacker for balance and executes a left hook kick to the attacker's midsection. (A left side sick can also be used here) NOTE: For control of the attacker's punching arm, the defender can grab the attacker's right arm after completing the block.

Scissor Throw (*Hasami Nage*) [Figures 3-4]

Fig. 3   After the hook kick, the defender goes down on both hands to prepare for the scissors throw.

Fig. 4   The defender places the right knee on the ground behind the attacker's right leg and fully extends the left leg in front of the attacker's lower abdomen.

Scissor Throw (*Hasami Nage*) [Figures 5-6]

Figs. 5-6   While maintaining the scissor position with the legs against the attacker's body, the defender then rotates his/her body counterclockwise forcing the attacker to fall backwards

Section 5 – Outer Major Sweep (*O Soto-gari*)

Outer Major Sweep (*O Soto-gari*) [Figures 1-3]

Figs. 1-2   The defender executes a left upper block against the attacker's right upper punch. The defender then grabs the attacker's arm with the left hand and pulls it down to the hip.

Fig. 3   The defender places the left foot forward outside of the attacker's right foot and at the same time strikes the attacker's jaw with the fleshy part of the outer side of the right palm.

Outer Major Sweep (*O Soto-gari*) [Figures 4-6]

Fig. 4   The defender brings the right foot forward in preparation for the sweep.

Figs. 5-6   The defender then sweeps the attacker's right leg using an arcing motion with his/her right foot on the floor, while simultaneously pushing the right hand against the attacker's jaw and pulling down on the attacker's right arm. A key point of the outer major sweep is the defender's right calf strikes the attacker's right calf, and the sweeping foot remains in contact with the floor.

ART AND THEORY OF SELF-DEFENSE | 199

Outer Major Sweep (*O Soto-gari*) [Figures 7-8]

Figs. 7-8 The defender continues to hold the attacker's right arm. If necessary, execute a finishing punch or kick (shown here) to the head.

Section 6 – Circular Block with Palm-Heel to Outer Major Sweep (*O Soto-gari*)

Circular Block to Palm-heel Strike to Chin and Outer Major Sweep (*O Soto-gari*) [Figures 1-2]

Figs. 1-2 Use an open-hand right circular block to parry the attacker's right upper punch.

Circular Block with Palm-Heel Strike to Outer Major Sweep (*O Soto-gari*) [Figures 3-5]

Fig. 3 Grab the attacking arm with the left hand, and push it down and inward. At the same time, perform a palm-heel strike to the attacker's chin. Step the left foot outside and next to the attacker's right foot.

Figs. 4-5 Sweep the attacker's right leg with the right leg while pushing the attacker's chin with the right hand and holding the attacker's left arm with the left hand. Synchronize the sweeping motion with the leg and pushing motion of the hand to make a throwing technique smooth and effective.

ART AND THEORY OF SELF-DEFENSE | 201

Circular Block with Palm-Heel Strike to Outer Major Sweep (*O Soto-gari*) [Figure 6]

Fig. 6   After completion of the sweep, an optional finishing technique may be executed as shown here, a punch to the attacker's temple.

Section 7 – Double-Wrist Grab from Behind to Wrist Throw (*Kotenage*)

Double-Wrist Grab from Behind to Wrist Throw (*Kotenage*) [Figures 1-2]

Figs. 1-2 Attacker grabs the wrists from behind. Defender lifts the left arm high, pivoting on the ball of the left foot, spin the body clockwise under the attacker's arm.

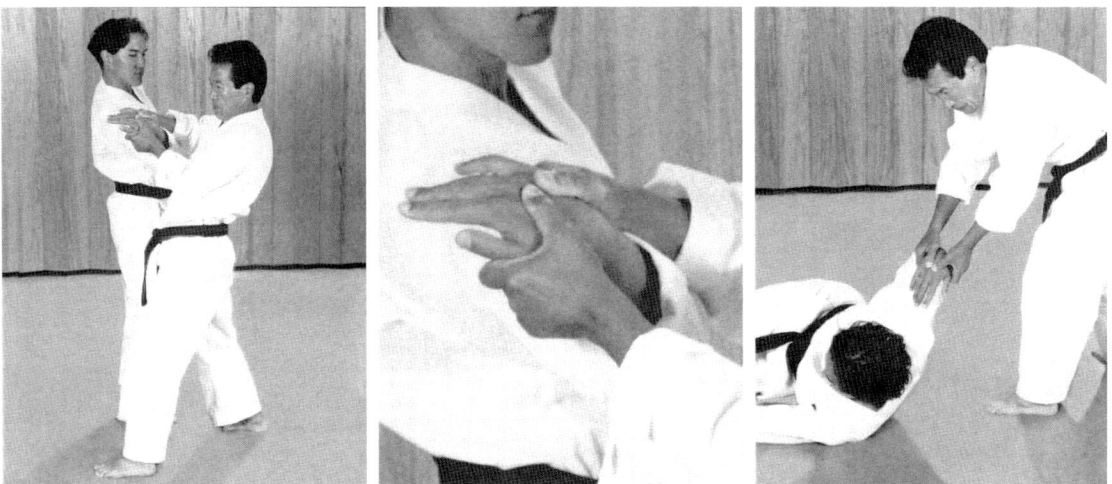

Double-Wrist Grab from Behind to Wrist Throw (*Kotenage*) [Figures 3-5]

Figs. 3-4 As the turn is completed, the attacker's left hand will release its hold. Immediately take control of the attacker's right hand as shown. (Be sure both thumbs are placed on the attacker's right hand on either side of the middle knuckle.)

Fig. 5 Twist the attacker's right hand back using both hands and step forward with the left foot continuing to apply pressure to the attacker's hand towards their wrist, twisting the hand backwards over the right side of the attacker's shoulder.

NOTE: In practice, take the attacker down gently, especially in the beginning for safety and better understanding of the technique. This technique can become a submission (holding method) as well, by keeping a hold on the attacker's hand and bending the wrist. Practice both sides, right and left

Section 8 – Ground Arm-bar Submission (*Kansetsu-waza*)

Ground Arm-bar Submission (*Kansetsu-waza*) [Figures 1-2]

Fig. 1   The defender executes a right upper block against the attacker's right upper punch.

Fig. 2   The defender grabs the attacker's right wrist with his/her right hand and pulls the arm downward.

Ground Arm-bar Submission (*Kansetsu-waza*) [Figures 3-4]

Fig. 3   The defender places the left foot outside of the attacker's right foot.

Fig. 4   The defender adjusts his/her right foot towards the left foot and brings the attacker's right wrist to the right hip.

Ground Arm-bar Submission (*Kansetsu-waza*) [Figures 5-6]

Fig. 5   The defender adjusts his/her feet by continuing to turn clockwise until the right foot is slightly in front of the left facing the same direction. At the same time, the defender places his/her left forearm approximately 1 inch above the attacker's right elbow joint outside the left while maintaining the hold of the attacker's right arm at the hip.

Fig. 6   The defender then sinks down on his/her left knee to take the attacker to the ground while applying pressure on the attacker's right elbow joint until the attacker is immobilized. It is important for the defender's toes of his/her right foot to be in-line with the attacker's forehead to create stability. The defender's left knee should be tight to the attacker's rib cage to help create a bridge with the attacker's arm between the shoulder and the defender's thigh.

NOTE: In practice, the attacker taps twice on the floor with the left hand to indicate submission.

CHAPTER 22

Defense from the Ground or Seated Position

You may be forced to defend yourself when you are lying on your stomach or back. If at all possible, try to get up on your feet at the first opportunity. However, if you are held down by the opponent, don't panic. With the power and strength in your lower stomach, use your legs to push or throw back the opponent. Use a loud *ki-ai*, which can give you more courage and strength.

Try to keep your head up all the time you are on the ground, and keep both knees fully bent. This "ready position" allows one to neutralize or counter an attack by an opponent. From this position one can parry a strike or throw the opponent backward, forward and even sideways. Try to get up on your feet as soon as you throw the opponent and gain control over the situation.

Another place that you may encounter an unwelcome advance or attack is on a bus, park bench or at a concert. A quick reaction to the aggression will be essential to getting away from the attacker.

Use every means possible to get away from your opponent. Don't hesitate to fight back by biting, spitting or scratching; although these techniques are not considered part of the traditional self-defense training, actual self-defense uses every available means.

Section 1 – Basic Posture for Ground Defense

Basic Ground Defense Posture [Figure 1]

Fig. 1   In a basic ground defense posture, the head is off the ground, and the arms are bent with elbows near chest. The knees are bent with the front of feet holding the ground. Using the power of the legs to roll onto one shoulder enables one to shift and to adjust the body in order to face a standing attacker if the attacker moves. From this basic posture, one can use the legs, knees and feet for protection or to attack.

HOW TO ASSUME BASIC GROUND DEFENSE POSTURE IN FORMAL PRACTICE

Assume Basic Ground Defense Posture in Formal Practice [Figures 1-2]

Figs. 1-2   From natural stance, slide the left foot to right foot and then step straight out with the right foot right and place the right hand on the ground in front of the right foot (as shown).

Assume Basic Ground Defense Posture in Formal Practice [Figures 3-4]

Figs. 3-4 Using right hand for support, swing right leg next to and past left foot to lower oneself to the ground with right leg straight and left knee bent. The hands are at the sides with the palms down and head off the floor.

Assume Basic Ground Defense Posture in Formal Practice [Figures 5-6]

Figs. 5-6 Then at the moment the attacker takes the "ready-to-attack" from a down block position (as shown), the defender's knees come up. In this position, the knees are near the chest and the hands come up directly off of the floor, so that the finger tips are pointed towards the ceiling but forearms and biceps are at a less than 90-degree angle.

Section 2 – Ground Defense Against a Standing Attacker with Knee Attack (*Hiza-kizushi*)

Ground Defense Against a Standing Attacker with Knee Attack (*Hiza-kizushi*) [Figures 1-2]

Figs. 1-2 The attacker steps in with the left foot forward into front stance and lunges towards the defender's face or throat. Parry away the attacker's hands using left foot striking at the elbow region of the attacker's right arm in a left to right motion.

Ground Defense Against a Standing Attacker with Knee Attack (*Hiza-kizushi*) [Figures 3-4]

Figs. 3-4 The right foot slides behind the attacker's right foot on the inside, so it is placed in between the attacker's legs, hooking the attacker's right ankle with the right foot.

Ground Defense Against a Standing Attacker with Knee Attack (*Hiza-kizushi*) [Figures 5-6]

Figs. 5-6 Put the bottom and blade of the left foot on the front of the attacker's right knee (just below the knee cap) and then take down the attacker by pushing with the left leg and pulling with the right leg.

Section 3 – Ground Defense Against A Choke

Ground Defense Against a Choke [Figures 1-2]

Fig. 1   While lying on the ground, the attacker tries to choke the defender. (In this case, assume the opponent is on the right side of the defender.)

Fig. 2   Tightly tuck and bring the right knee up to strike the attacker's stomach or ribs. Weaken the choke by grabbing the attacker's wrists or thumbs.

Ground Defense Against a Choke [Figures 3-4]

Fig. 3   The defender grabs the attacker's arms, brings the right leg inside and pushes the attacker away with the right leg. Use the strength and support of the left leg by keeping the left foot on the ground.

Fig. 4   Kick the attacker's chin with the right foot to stun the attacker.

Ground Defense Against a Choke [Figures 5-7]

Figs. 5-7 Finish breaking the attacker's hold by straightening the right leg and striking the attacker's right arm with the right leg. Escape by rolling away to left.

NOTE: Practice this from the other side as well with the attacker coming from the left side.

Section 4 - Defense from Seated Position: Basic Technique

Defense From a Seated Position: Variation One [Figures 1-3]

Fig. 1   While sitting in a chair, an attacker attempts to choke the defender from behind. Bring the right foot back slightly so that it's closer to the attacker. Raise the hands up, palms facing inward.

Fig. 2   Rise off the chair and turn clockwise towards the attacker. Turn the palms of hands away, parrying the attacker's choking arm from the neck. Feel power in the lower abdomen (*tanden*), using the strength of the lower abdomen and hips to release the hold.

Fig. 3   Move the left foot to the side of the chair and then pull the right foot around to line up with the left foot. At the same time, grab the attacker's arm with the right hand while pulling it firmly to the right hip and place the left forearm just above the attacker's elbow.

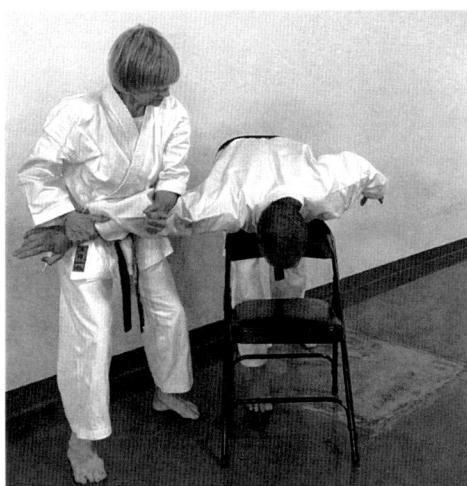 

Defense From a Seated Position: Variation One [Figures 4-5]

Figs. 4-5   While securing the attacker's right arm against the hip, continue to turn clockwise while pressing on their elbow with the left forearm. Exert pressure on the elbow until the attacker is immobilized with their abdomen pushed against the back of the chair. Continue with the downward pressure on the arm, while sliding the elbow to strike the attacker's head

APPENDIX and BIBLIOGRAPHY

Appendix – New York State Penal Code   P. 217

Bibliography   P. 223

Appendix – New York State Penal Code - ARTICLE 35

The following text was published by the New York State Legislature on their website. The link used to access the text was: http://public.leginfo.state.ny.us/lawssrch.cgi?NVLWO

ARTICLE 35   DEFENSE OF JUSTIFICATION

Section 35.00 Justification; a defense.
      35.05 Justification; generally.
      35.10 Justification; use of physical force generally.
      35.15 Justification; use of physical force in defense of a person.
      35.20 Justification; use of physical force in defense of premises and in defense of a person in the course of burglary.
      35.25 Justification; use of physical force to prevent or terminate larceny or criminal mischief.
      35.27 Justification; use of physical force in resisting arrest prohibited.
      35.30 Justification; use of physical force in making an arrest or in preventing an escape.

---

§ 35.00 Justification; a defense.

In any prosecution for an offense, justification, as defined in sections 35.05 through 35.30, is a defense.

§ 35.05 Justification; generally.

Unless otherwise limited by the ensuing provisions of this article defining justifiable use of physical force, conduct which would otherwise constitute an offense is justifiable and not criminal when:
1. Such conduct is required or authorized by law or by a judicial decree, or is performed by a public servant in the reasonable exercise of his official powers, duties or functions; or
2. Such conduct is necessary as an emergency measure to avoid an imminent public or private injury which is about to occur by reason of a situation occasioned or developed through no fault of the actor, and which is of such gravity that, according to ordinary standards of intelligence and morality, the desirability and urgency of avoiding such injury clearly outweigh the desirability of avoiding the injury sought to be prevented by the statute defining the offense in issue. The necessity and justifiability of such conduct may not rest upon considerations pertaining only to the morality and advisability of the statute, either in its general application or with respect to its application to a particular class of cases arising thereunder. Whenever evidence relating to the defense of justification under this subdivision is offered by the defendant, the court shall rule as a matter of law whether the claimed facts and circumstances would, if established, constitute a defense.

§ 35.10 Justification; use of physical force generally.

The use of physical force upon another person which would otherwise constitute an offense is justifiable and not criminal under any of the following circumstances:

1. A parent, guardian or other person entrusted with the care and supervision of a person under the age of twenty-one or an incompetent person, and a teacher or other person entrusted with the care and supervision of a person under the age of twenty-one for a special purpose, may use physical force, but not deadly physical force, upon such person when and to the extent that he reasonably believes it necessary to maintain discipline or to promote the welfare of such person.

2. A warden or other authorized official of a jail, prison or correctional institution may, in order to maintain order and discipline, use such physical force as is authorized by the correction law.

3. A person responsible for the maintenance of order in a common carrier of passengers, or a person acting under his direction, may use physical force when and to the extent that he reasonably believes it necessary to maintain order, but he may use deadly physical force only when he reasonably believes it necessary to prevent death or serious physical injury.

4. A person acting under a reasonable belief that another person is about to commit suicide or to inflict serious physical injury upon himself may use physical force upon such person to the extent that he reasonably believes it necessary to thwart such result.

5. A duly licensed physician, or a person acting under a physician's direction, may use physical force for the purpose of administering a recognized form of treatment which he or she reasonably believes to be adapted to promoting the physical or mental health of the patient if (a) the treatment is administered with the consent of the patient or, if the patient is under the age of eighteen years or an incompetent person, with the consent of the parent, guardian or other person entrusted with the patient's care and supervision, or (b) the treatment is administered in an emergency when the physician reasonably believes that no one competent to consent can be consulted and that a reasonable person, wishing to safeguard the welfare of the patient, would consent.

6. A person may, pursuant to the ensuing provisions of this article, use physical force upon another person in self-defense or defense of a third person, or in defense of premises, or in order to prevent larceny of or criminal mischief to property, or in order to effect an arrest or prevent an escape from custody. Whenever a person is authorized by any such provision to use deadly physical force in any given circumstance, nothing contained in any other such provision may be deemed to negate or qualify such authorization.

35.15 Justification; use of physical force in defense of a person.

1. A person may, subject to the provisions of subdivision two, use physical force upon another person when and to the extent he or she reasonably believes such to be necessary to defend himself, herself or a third person from what he or she reasonably believes to be the use or imminent use of unlawful physical force by such other person, unless:

(a) The latter's conduct was provoked by the actor with intent to cause physical injury to another person; or

(b) The actor was the initial aggressor; except that in such case the use of physical force is nevertheless justifiable if the actor has withdrawn from the encounter and effectively communicated such withdrawal to such other person but the latter persists in continuing the incident by the use or threatened imminent use of unlawful physical force; or

(c) The physical force involved is the product of a combat by agreement not specifically authorized by law.

2. A person may not use deadly physical force upon another person under circumstances specified in subdivision one unless:

(a) The actor reasonably believes that such other person is using or about to use deadly physical force. Even in such case, however, the actor may not use deadly physical force if he or she knows that with complete personal safety, to oneself and others he or she may avoid the necessity of so doing by retreating; except that the actor is under no duty to retreat if he or she is:

(i) in his or her dwelling and not the initial aggressor; or

(ii) a police officer or peace officer or a person assisting a police officer or a peace officer at the latter's direction, acting pursuant to section 35.30; or

(b) He or she reasonably believes that such other person is committing or attempting to commit a kidnapping, forcible rape, forcible criminal sexual act or robbery; or

(c) He or she reasonably believes that such other person is committing or attempting to commit a burglary, and the circumstances are such that the use of deadly physical force is authorized by subdivision three of section 35.20.

§ 35.20 Justification; use of physical force in defense of premises and in defense of a person in the course of burglary.

1. Any person may use physical force upon another person when he or she reasonably believes such to be necessary to prevent or terminate what he or she reasonably believes to be the commission or attempted commission by such other person of a crime involving damage to premises. Such person may use any degree of physical force, other than deadly physical force, which he or she reasonably believes to be necessary for such purpose, and may use deadly physical force if he or she reasonably believes such to be necessary to prevent or terminate the commission or attempted commission of arson.

2. A person in possession or control of any premises, or a person licensed or privileged to be thereon or therein, may use physical force upon another person when he or she reasonably believes such to be necessary to prevent or terminate what he or she reasonably believes to be the commission or attempted commission by such other person of a criminal trespass upon such premises. Such person may use any degree of physical force, other than deadly physical force, which he or she reasonably believes to be necessary for such purpose, and may use deadly physical force in order to prevent or terminate the commission or attempted commission of arson, as prescribed in subdivision one, or in the course of a burglary or attempted burglary, as prescribed in subdivision three.

3. A person in possession or control of, or licensed or privileged to be in, a dwelling or an occupied building, who reasonably believes that another person is committing or attempting to commit a burglary of such dwelling or building, may use deadly physical force upon such other person when he or she reasonably believes such to be necessary to prevent or terminate the commission or attempted commission of such burglary.

4. As used in this section, the following terms have the following meanings:

(a) The terms "premises," "building" and "dwelling" have the meanings prescribed in section 140.00;

(b) Persons "licensed or privileged" to be in buildings or upon other premises include, but are not limited to:

(i) police officers or peace officers acting in the performance of their duties; and

(ii) security personnel or employees of nuclear powered electric generating facilities located within the state who are employed as part of any security plan approved by the federal operating license agencies acting in the performance of their duties at such generating facilities. For purposes of this subparagraph, the term "nuclear powered electric generating facility" shall mean a facility that generates electricity using nuclear power for sale, directly or indirectly, to the public, including the land upon which the facility is located and the safety and security zones as defined under federal regulations.

§ 35.25 Justification; use of physical force to prevent or terminate larceny or criminal mischief.

A person may use physical force, other than deadly physical force, upon another person when and to the extent that he or she reasonably believes such to be necessary to prevent or terminate what he or she reasonably believes to be the commission or attempted commission by such other person of larceny or of criminal mischief with respect to property other than premises.

§ 35.27 Justification; use of physical force in resisting arrest prohibited.

A person may not use physical force to resist an arrest, whether authorized or unauthorized, which is being effected or attempted by a police officer or peace officer when it would reasonably appear that the latter is a police officer or peace officer.

§ 35.30 Justification; use of physical force in making an arrest or in preventing an escape.

1. A police officer or a peace officer, in the course of effecting or attempting to effect an arrest, or of preventing or attempting to prevent the escape from custody, of a person whom he or she reasonably believes to have committed an offense, may use physical force when and to the extent he or she reasonably believes such to be necessary to effect the arrest, or to prevent the escape from custody, or in self-defense or to defend a third person from what he or she reasonably believes to be the use or imminent use of physical force; except that deadly physical force may be used for such purposes only when he or she reasonably believes that:
(a) The offense committed by such person was:
(i) a felony or an attempt to commit a felony involving the use or attempted use or threatened imminent use of physical force against a person; or
(ii) kidnapping, arson, escape in the first degree, burglary in the first degree or any attempt to commit such a crime; or
(b) The offense committed or attempted by such person was a felony and that, in the course of resisting arrest therefor or attempting to escape from custody, such person is armed with a firearm or deadly weapon; or
(c) Regardless of the particular offense which is the subject of the arrest or attempted escape, the use of deadly physical force is necessary to defend the police officer or peace officer or another person from what the officer reasonably believes to be the use or imminent use of deadly physical force.
2. The fact that a police officer or a peace officer is justified in using deadly physical force under circumstances prescribed in paragraphs (a) and (b) of subdivision one does not constitute justification for reckless conduct by such police officer or peace officer amounting to an offense against or with respect to innocent persons whom he or she is not seeking to arrest or retain in custody.
3. A person who has been directed by a police officer or a peace officer to assist such police officer or peace officer to effect an arrest or to prevent an escape from custody may use physical force, other than deadly physical force, when and to the extent that he or she

reasonably believes such to be necessary to carry out such police officer's or peace officer's direction, unless he or she knows that the arrest or prospective arrest is not or was not authorized and may use deadly physical force under such circumstances when:

(a) He or she reasonably believes such to be necessary for self-defense or to defend a third person from what he or she reasonably believes to be the use or imminent use of deadly physical force; or

(b) He or she is directed or authorized by such police officer or peace officer to use deadly physical force unless he or she knows that the police officer or peace officer is not authorized to use deadly physical force under the circumstances.

4. A private person acting on his or her own account may use physical force, other than deadly physical force, upon another person when and to the extent that he or she reasonably believes such to be necessary to effect an arrest or to prevent the escape from custody of a person whom he or she reasonably believes to have committed an offense and who in fact has committed such offense; and may use deadly physical force for such purpose when he or she reasonably believes such to be necessary to:

(a) Defend himself, herself or a third person from what he or she reasonably believes to be the use or imminent use of deadly physical force; or

(b) Effect the arrest of a person who has committed murder, manslaughter in the first degree, robbery, forcible rape or forcible criminal sexual act and who is in immediate flight therefrom.

5. A guard, police officer or peace officer who is charged with the duty of guarding prisoners in a detention facility, as that term is defined in section 205.00, or while in transit to or from a detention facility, may use physical force when and to the extent that he or she reasonably believes such to be necessary to prevent the escape of a prisoner from a detention facility or from custody while in transit thereto or therefrom.

Bibliography

- Carroll, Scott T.: "Wrestling in Ancient Nubia", Journal of Sport History, Vol. 15, No. 2 (Summer, 1988).

- "FAQ." ENGLISH GUIDE, Nippon Budokan, 2016, www.nipponbudokan.or.jp/english.

- Frachetti, Michael D., et al. "Nomadic Ecology Shaped the Highland Geography of Asia's Silk Roads." Nature News, Nature Publishing Group, 8 Mar. 2017, www.nature.com/articles/nature21696.

- Henning, Stanley E. "China Review International." China Review International, Vol. 5, No. 2, 1998, pp. 417–424. JSTOR, JSTOR, www.jstor.org/stable/23732360.

- Herrigel, Eugen. *Zen*. New York: McGraw-Hill, 1964. Print.

- Hume, Robert Ernest. *The Thirteen Principal Upanishads: Translated from the Sanskrit with an Outline of the Philosophy of the Upanishads and an Annotated Bibliography*, Oxford University Press, 1921.

- Hessbruegge, Jan Arno. *Human Rights and Personal Self-Defense in International Law*. Oxford University Press, 2017. eBook.

- Kochanek, Kenneth D, et al. "Deaths: Final Data for 2014." *National Vital Statistics Reports*, vol. 65, no. 4, 2016, pp. 1, 2 and 5., www.cdc.gov/nchs/data/nvsr/nvsr65/nvsr65_04.pdf.

- Laozi, Tzu, Lao. *Tao Te Ching*, translated by Arthur Waley, Wordsworth Editions Limited, 1997.

- Laozi, and William Scott Wilson. *Tao Te Ching: An All-New Translation*, Shambhala, 2013.

- Lorge, Peter Allan. Chinese Martial Arts: from Antiquity to the Twenty-First Century. Cambridge University Press, 2012.

- Meyer, Milton Walter. *Asia: A Concise History*. Lanham, MD: Rowman & Littlefield, 1997. Print.

- Milman, Henry Hart, and Williams, Monier. *Story of Nala: An Episode of the Mahabharata*. Oxford: UP, 1860. Print.

- Miyamoto, Musashi. *A Way to Victory: The Annotated Book of Five Rings*. Trans. Hidy Ochiai. New York: Overlook, 2005. Print.

- Moffitt, Terrie E. "A Gradient of Childhood Self-Control Predicts Health, Wealth, and Public Safety." Proceedings of the National Academy of Sciences of the United States of America, National Academy of Sciences, 15 Feb. 2011, www.ncbi.nlm.nih.gov/pmc/articles/PMC3041102/.

- Nagamine, Shoshin. Trans. Patrick McCarthy. *Tales of Okinawa's Great Masters*. Boston: Tuttle Pub., 2000. Print.

- Nair, Sreenath. *Restoration of Breath: Consciousness and Performance*. Amsterdam: Rodopi, 2007. Print.

- "Newberry, Percy E. : Beni Hasan (Band 2) (London, 1893)." Vereinigung Bildender Künstler Österreichs Secession [Hrsg.]: Ver Sacrum: Mittheilungen Der Vereinigung Bildender Künstler Österreichs (1.1898), University of Heidelberg, 2012, digi.ub.uni-heidelberg.de/diglit/newberry1893bd2/0105/image.

- Oaten, Megan, and Ken Cheng. "Longitudinal Gains in Self-regulation from Regular Physical Exercise." *British Journal of Health Psychology* 11.4 (2006): 717-33. US National Library of Medicine. Web. 4 Jan. 2017. https://www.ncbi.nlm.nih.gov/pubmed/17032494.

- Plato. *Plato in Twelve Volumes, Vol. 9* translated by Harold N. Fowler. Cambridge, MA, Harvard University Press; London, William Heinemann Ltd. 1925. The Annenberg CPB/Project. http://www.perseus.tufts.edu/hopper/text?doc=Perseus%3Atext%3A1999.01.0174%3Atext%3DPhileb.%3Asection%3D58d

- Rasmussen M, Li Y, Lindgreen ST et al (2010) "Ancient Human Genome Sequence of an Extinct Palaeo-Eskimo". *Nature*. 463(7282): 757-62.

- Sangero, Boaz. *Introduction. Self-Defence in Criminal Law* (Criminal Law Library; v. 1). N.p.: Hart Limited, 2006. Print.

- Sastri, Alladi Mahadeva. *The Yoga-Upanishads*. Madras: Adyar Library, 1938. Print.

- Soseki, Muso, and Thomas Yuho Kirchner. *Dialogues in a Dream: The Life and Zen Teachings of Muso Soseki*, Wisdom Publications, 2015.

- Tzu, Sun, and Thomas F. Cleary. *The Art of War*. Boston, MA: Shambhala, 2005. 27. Print.

- Tzu, Sun, and Thomas Cleary. *The Art of War: Complete Texts and Commentaries*, Shambhala Publications, 2005.

- "What You Need to Know about Willpower: The Psychological Science of Self-Control." *American Psychological Association*, 2012. Web. 04 Jan. 2017. http://www.apa.org/helpcenter/willpower.pdf.

- Wickett, Elizabeth. "Archaeological Memory, the Leitmotifs of Ancient Egyptian Festival Tradition, and Cultural Legacy in the Festival Tradition of Luxor: the Mulid of Sidi Abu'l Hajjaj Al-Uqsori and the Ancient Egyptian 'Feast of Opet.'" Journal of the American Research Center in Egypt, vol. 45, 2009, pp. 403–426. JSTOR, JSTOR, www.jstor.org/stable/25735464.

- Wilkinson, Toby A. H. *Early Dynastic Egypt*, Routledge, 2005, pp. 56-57

- Wilkinson, John Gardner. *A Popular Account of the Ancient Egyptians. from His Larger Work*, by Sir J. Gardner Wilkinson. Illustrated with Five Hundred Woodcuts. Vol. 1, J. Murray, 1874.

- Zhuangzi. *Complete Works of Zhuangzi,* trans. Burton Watson, Columbia Univ. Press, 2013.

Worksheet 1

Name: _____

Semester: _____

1. Why is it valuable to teach a "school appropriate" self-defense program to children? What is the highest aim of a true student of self-defense?

2. What is the definition of non-violence, and how is it essential to the study of self-defense? How do children learn to make a choice of peace?

3. What character traits and techniques/skills would enable one to "win without fighting"? Mention specific qualities and methods described in the text.

Worksheet 2

Name: _____

Semester: _____

1. Define two kinds of seeing—*Ken* and *Kan*.

2. Describe how these types of seeing apply to each of the levels of self-defense.

   Level One:

   Level Two:

   Level Three:

3. What positive character traits can be developed through self-defense training? What can be described as the upward spiral of self-development?

Worksheet 3

Name: _____

Semester: _____

1. What are six key elements for developing a proper attitude in self-defense training? List and explain key element.

2. How do breathing techniques help the mind prepare for training and what is *mokuso*?

3. What is *ki-ai*? What is the purpose of *ki-ai*? How could the practice of *ki-ai* help a shy child develop self-confidence?

Worksheet 4

Name: _____

Semester: _____

1. What are the four major stances that are taught in the mind-body connection and what does each stance signify?

2. Why is it important to strengthen the mind-body connection through constant practice?

3. What is *zan-shin* and why is it important in self-defense practice and applied to character education?

Worksheet 5

Name: _____

Semester: _____

1. Describe how to make a proper (self-defense) fist.
   Describe the key elements of proper punching technique.

2. What is known as the "ethical principle of self-defense"?
   In relation to this principle, why is blocking always taught before punching or kicking?

3. How does learning the art of self-defense punching and striking contribute to an increased sense of self-empowerment?

Worksheet 6

Name: _____

Semester: _____

1. What is *kata*?
   Explain why kata is more than just going through the motions.
   Give three reasons *kata* practice is and essential part of learning self-defense.

2. Describe the four key elements proper kicking technique?

3. When executing a kick, why it is important to pull back the kicking leg
   (in the same line) as hard if not harder as the actual kick itself? Explain.

Worksheet 7

Name: _____

Semester: _____

1. What is *ukemi*? What is most important when practicing *ukemi*?

2. Describe the important points of the following:

    - Back Fall

    - Side Fall (left and right sides)

    - Front Fall

3. How can you teach a modified form *ukemi* to young children?

Worksheet 8

Name: _____

Semester: _____

1. Within the theory of "Situational Self-Defense" practice, describe what is known as the grammar of self-defense?

2. What are the fundamental elements of self-defense techniques?

   Describe why these fundamental elements are emphasized in the practice of self-defense techniques?

3. What is a "stunning technique" in self-defense?

   In what circumstance would an elbow strike, a back-fist strike or a low kick be useful as a stunning technique?

Worksheet 9

Name: _____

Semester: _____

1. How would a "Self-defense Creed" help in teaching a school class in self-defense?

2. What is Shoshin and What is Kaizen? How can these concepts help in teaching a school class in self-defense?

Worksheet 10

Name: _____

1. There are four STORY INSTERTS, which are highlighted in the first five chapters of this text. Historically, these kinds of tales are told to students in order to augment their learning in a practical manner.

   Explain the lessons or morals of each story.

Semester: _____

2. Which story did you like most and why?